TRIVIA CHALLENGES

The Little Book of Fun Filled Trivia Choices

GARY D PALMER

Trivia Challenges
Copyright © 2019 by Gary D Palmer

All rights reserved. No part of this publication may be reproduced, distributed, or transmitted in any form or by any means, including photocopying, recording, or other electronic or mechanical methods, without the prior written permission of the author, except in the case of brief quotations embodied in critical reviews and certain other non-commercial uses permitted by copyright law.

Tellwell Talent
www.tellwell.ca

ISBN
978-0-2288-0990-6 (Paperback)
978-0-2288-0991-3 (eBook)

How good are you at separating fact from fiction? Are you up on your trivia? This little book is here to help you test your trivia skills, and to allow you to have a little fun while doing so. Test your friends, test your family or perhaps test just yourself. Each question which follows has a number of possible answers. See if you can pick the correct one from among all of the others (which may sound correct but are actually pure fiction). Keep in mind that what appears at first glance to be completely logical may not be the way it really "was."

The Questions Commence

Answers may be found beginning on page 117

ONE

If someone is said to be "punch drunk", does that mean he or she...

1. got tipsy from drinking the spiked fruit punch at a social?

2. was a professional boxer who was hit in the head so many times that now his or her brains are addled?

3. is acting like "Punch" from the old "Punch and Judy" puppet shows in which Punch was normally depicted as being inebriated?

4. has become addicted to beating up people?

TWO

Julius Caesar, after returning from his victories in Gaul (modern day France), was commanded by the Roman Senate to leave his troops at the Rubicon River before entering Rome. They feared his growing popularity and power. Caesar feared for his safety if he were to enter Rome without his troops. He finally decided to cross the river with his soldiers. As he did so, it is claimed he said, "The die is cast". (or was it "the dye is cast.")?

This means:

1. He has thrown the dice, and you cannot "unthrow" them. Whatever the results of this defiance, he was going to have to live with it.

2. The dye has been placed in with the clothes. and they cannot be uncoloured. Whatever the results of this defiance, he was going to have to live with it.

3. The molten metal has been poured into the mould and it is now too late to reshape it. Whatever the results of this defiance, he was going to have to live with it.

4. He had troops who died serving under him. If you die serving your leader you expect that leader to continue to lead. In effect they voted for him, and he felt it incumbent upon him to honor those deaths. Whatever the results of this defiance, he was going to have to live with it.

THREE

Have you ever had a clerk or someone say to you, "I'll be with you in a moment?" Many don't realize it, but they are actually giving reference to a specific time measurement. A moment is...

1. 60 seconds. The phrase is actually a corruption of the phrase, "I'll be with you in a minute."

2. the time between the beats of a heart. The phrase could be better said, "I'll be with you in a heartbeat."

3. immeasurable. A moment actually refers to a position in time that is so infinitesimally small that it cannot be measured.

4. 90 seconds. This dates back to the Middle Ages when it was determined that there were 40 moments in an hour.

FOUR

World War One. Canada entered the war ill-prepared to wage any sort of a war. By the end of the conflict, however, the world found that Canada had fielded a significant fighting force. During the last 100 days of the War the Canadian Corps (4 Divisions strong) had...

1. Defeated or put to flight 47 German divisions, taken approximately 32,000 German prisoners, and captured approximately 3800 German artillery pieces, heavy machine guns and mortars.

2. Defeated or put to flight 23 German divisions, taken approximately 16,000 German prisoners and captured approximately 1600 German artillery pieces, heavy machine guns and mortars.

3. Defeated or put to flight 5 German Divisions, taken approximately 2000 German prisoners and captured approximately 300 German artillery pieces, heavy machine guns and mortars.

4. This is a trick question. Canada had fought well at battles such as Vimy earlier in the war, but the German Spring Offensive of 1918 had mauled them so severely that by the end of the war they were still in no condition to do much fighting, and, instead, acted more as support troops for the American forces that had largely replaced them at the front.

FIVE

We've all said good bye to someone. Do you know what kind of wishes you have, in reality, extended to that someone?

1. You have actually extended your hopes that God accompanies them on their journey. The phrase actually began as "God be with you. Over time it gradually morphed into "God be wi' ye", into "God b'wy." and finally, "Good bye."

2. Good bye has always meant good bye, although people have gradually forgot what "bye" is. That now obsolete term once referred to those daylight hours between morning and afternoon, roughly from 10:00 am to 2:00 pm. Consequently, "Good bye" fits right in with its cousins, "Good morning", "Good afternoon", "Good evening", and "Good night."

3. "Good bye" was once "Good by" and meant "May you find good lodgings enroute." In the days when all roads were country roads, and trips of even a few miles often necessitated an overnight stay at some inn somewhere on your journey, travel on the "by-ways" of England could be uncertain and hazardous, with accommodations varying greatly in quality.

4. In the Middle Ages travel by common folk was usually extremely limited and restricted to those of the male persuasion. Parents and family members bidding farewell to these individuals would often offer a quick bit of advice as they did so. The simple phrase "Good boy" translated

into "behave yourself as you travel." Over time a slight modification took place with "good boy" transforming itself into "good b'y" or "good bye," with the "good boy" connection to the term eventually forgotten.

SIX

Have you ever purchased anything on sale? The answer to that is likely, "yes." Next question: Do you know the origin of the word "sale?"

1. It's of 18th Century Origin. Textiles being imported into England were cheaper than those British made, but of inferior quality. Merchants selling these textiles identified them as imports by noting how they came into the country. "By Sail" or "By Sale" (either spelling was considered appropriate at the time) which was later abbreviated to simply "Sail" or "Sale".

2. British tourists visiting France noticed that French merchants would often sell shopworn or slightly damaged goods for discounted prices. The tables upon which they were displayed were labeled "salé", which is the French word for "soiled" or "dirty". Most of these tourists had no idea what the word meant, but they recognized a bargain when they saw one, and liked the concept. British merchants began to follow suit. They also labeled their bargain goods as "salé", although without the accented "e".

3. The word "sale" has actually been around for ages. It is derived from the Norse word "sala", entered English in that form, and was later modernized to "sale". It's meaning was simply "to sell". The word's use in a sense of "a selling of shop goods at lower prices than usual" first appeared in 1866.

4. The word originated in the London dockside fish markets. In the early 19th Century they began standardizing prices, and largely eliminated the old practice of haggling. Set prices became the norm, although shoppers could save if they were willing to make do with slightly older catches. To differentiate it from the fresher product, sellers would label such packages as "Seafood Approaching Legal Expiry." It was too cumbersome, of course, to use the full phrase, so merchants quickly came to the realization that something shorter was required. Using just the initials — S.A.L.E.— proved a quick and easy solution. Purchasers didn't always know what the letters meant. They just knew that the purchase was a Sale item. The use of the term soon spread beyond the fish markets.

5. The word arose as a typo in 1854. A prominent London baker decided to promote his day old bread which still could be used in various forms at mealtime. He ordered several signs from a local printer that simply read "STALE". He intended to place these on the tables displaying his discounted product. However, they came back from the printer reading "SALE." Needing something, the bakery decided to use them until corrections could be made and the proper product delivered. This strange new word drew the attention of the owner's customers. The baked goods sold briskly, so well, in fact, that the baker decided to keep the old signs and forget about having them replaced. It wasn't long before other nearby merchants were having their own "sales." The idea, of course, soon spread far afield.

SEVEN

You have probably all heard how Canadian and American pioneers were often referred to as homesteaders. Generally, homesteaders received land grants, and in return for working that land were eventually granted title to it. So, what's the mystery? Well, "home" is a pretty common term, but what is a "stead"?

1. This comes from the old English term "hamstede" and simply refers to the land upon which your home has been built. It could be farmland, a city plot, anywhere where your primary dwelling has been constructed.

2. Yes, "hamstede" is the term. "Ham" does translate as "home". "Stead" refers to "a lot of land adequate for the maintenance of a family" This was generally accepted to be 160 acres.

3. Well, yes, "hamstede" is the correct term, but "ham" does not quite mean "home". It means "habitable land upon which a home could be built". "Stead" refers to the fact that it is government owned, or, going back to its feudal origins, part of the "royal domains."

4. "Stead" actually has nothing at all to do with land use. It is property which has been "zoned" for the building of outbuildings, although its use is old and predates that term "zone". It also does not necessarily relate to all of the property owned by an individual. It sometimes applies to only a portion of that property.

EIGHT

Another trivia question—one not based on definitions, but one based on historical fact. Back in the 13th and 14th centuries the disease known as "The Black Death", the bubonic plague, swept the known world. It was so widespread, so severe, and so deadly that a minimum of 30%, but perhaps as much as 60%, of the population of Europe was killed by it. Repercussions, as might be expected, were huge.

Most scientists now believe the plague was the result of …

1. the bites of infected fleas.

2. the bites of infected rats.

3. scratches and bites inflicted by half-crazed, infected cats.

4. simple contact with infected pigs, with the plague being a particularly virulent form of swine flu.

NINE

We often hear about the "hat trick". This, of course, is a hockey term referring to a three goal night for some skilled player, who had a particularly good game. So, you know what a hat trick is, but do you how the term originated?

Does it date back to...

1. 1947. when a newly recruited NHL hockey player admired a particularly nice fedora in a haberdasher's shop. This was a time when hockey players were not well paid, and the rookie player simply couldn't afford to buy it. The hat maker, who was a hockey fan himself. told the young player that if he scored three goals in that night's game he would give him the hat. He did and he did. The story soon spread, and henceforth a three goal game was known as a "hat trick."

2. 1936. A radio announcer, during a break in the play, just happened to tell a little story about the little game of flicking a deck of cards, one card at a time, across a room and into a hat lying on the floor. It is extremely unusual to get the whole deck into the hat without missing with at least a few cards. It takes a skillful flick and a fair amount of luck to be successful. Once play resumed, and shortly thereafter, one of the players scored his third goal of the night. The announcer's comment: "Now there's a real hat trick for you!" The name stuck.

3. 1927. A Toronto Maple Leaf player, normally a team leader when it came to goal scoring, accuracy of his passing, and outplaying his opponents, had just had a very bad night characterized by broken sticks, missed opportunities, and sloppy play. After the game a newspaper reporter asked him what had gone wrong. His answer was a surprising one. He said that he had forgot to wear his lucky hat to the game. He promised to never make that mistake again. The next game he, indeed, remembered to wear his hat, and had a remarkable game, scoring three goals. The reporter, of course, reported upon the player's "hat trick."

4. 1856. "Hat trick," actually did not originate as a hockey term. It originated as a cricket term. During league play in England one player actually took three wickets in three consecutive deliveries, a remarkable achievement. Appreciative fans held a collection for him, and presented the team hero with a hat bought with the proceeds. Hence, the "hat trick." Years later, hockey (and other sports) commandeered the term.

TEN

Born: 24-Mar-1887
Image from: http://www.nndb.com/people/028/000031932/

More historic trivia.

Did you ever hear of Fatty Arbuckle? If you said, "No," then you are probably not alone. Hardly anyone is familiar with the name, yet he once was one of the most popular, most powerful, and certainly highest paid star in Hollywood. In 1921 this comedy genius signed a million dollar, three-year contract with Paramount—an unheard of amount at the time, even in Hollywood. Yet, not long after this his career came to an abrupt end, so abrupt that today he is scarcely remembered. So what happened to Fatty Arbuckle?

1. Shortly after signing his contract he started a new picture, one in which the flying of airplanes was a prominent part. Fatty didn't have to do much flying himself; that was left to the stuntmen, with most of his scenes being filmed on the ground. Nevertheless, he thought this would be the perfect opportunity to see what it was like to fly, and asked one of the bi-plane pilots if he would mind "taking him up". The pilot, as might be expected, was more than willing. The short little, test flight, however, ended tragically. While trying to impress his famous passenger, the aviator flew a little too low, clipped a telephone line, which caused the plane to flip, and both men were killed in the resulting crash.

2. Shortly after signing his contract, Fatty and a few of his friends arranged a lavish dinner party to celebrate. During the course of the party a young starlet was found nearly naked and unconscious on the floor of one of the suites. Accusations were made against the prominent comedian, saying that he had taken advantage of his inebriated guest, raping her, and, because of the violence of the act and his massive weight, leaving her not only violated but nearly suffocated. She, in fact, later died. Fatty ended up being tried for manslaughter. He was acquitted, with the jury being adamant in asserting that he should never have been charged, and that there was absolutely no evidence to link him with the death. He was innocent, but the damage had been done. He was now being blacklisted by the Hollywood establishment, and his career was not only in tatters, but over.

3. In the days of the silent movie, humour was mostly visual, and Fatty was very adept in using his weight to his advantage when it came to that humour. It was one of the things that brought him fame and fortune. He found, however, that his weight also presented some disadvantages. In

1924, at the relativity young age of 37, the 300 pound comedian suffered a massive heart attack. He was immediately hospitalized, but never recovered, dying in his hospital bed.

4. The `talkies` did him in. In reality he had a rather high pitched, squeaky voice. This didn`t matter when the movie was made without sound, but when the silent movie era came to an end, he found that his voice was very much a detriment to him. Audiences were still laughing, but now it was at him rather than with him. It quickly became evident that his career was now over. Fatty took an early and unplanned retirement. The fortune he had made allowed him to retire in comfort, but his sudden departure from the Hollywood scene caused audiences to soon forget the name of Fatty Arbuckle.

5. Fatty and Charlie Chaplin, another megastar, had once been friends, but a minor disagreement between the two soon turned into a major rupture, with accusations being thrown back and forth, with both men charging the other with copyright infringement. Lawyers became involved, lawsuits were issued, and, it seems Charlie had the better set of attorneys. Charlie Chaplin won and his name and his star continued to shine in Hollywood history. Fatty Arbuckle lost and his name effectively disappeared from Hollywood history.

6. In 1925 Fatty came to the stunning decision that he didn`t want to do comedies anymore. He wanted to expand his horizons. He wanted to change from a comedic star to a dramatic star. He now refused to accept any comedy roles. It was a big mistake. His foray into drama fizzled. It turns out he was as bad a dramatic actor as he was a great comedy actor. By the time he realized his error it was too late. Certainly, and with good reason, no one

was offering him any serious roles, and now no one was offering him any comedy roles either. He had unintentionally scuttled his own career.

Okay, six choices this time instead of the usual four.

ELEVEN

"Fake News".

The U.S. President, Donald Trump, has made frequent use of this term, accusing formerly (?) respected news agencies of purposely claiming things to be true that they know to be false, usually in an attempt to attack him. Is this something new. If not, who first began to cite "fake news?"

1. Yes, this is, indeed, true. Propaganda has been around for a long time, but never before have such accusations been applied to news sources that are at least theoretically unbiased and whose conclusions are said to be based on fact and not fiction. Whether he is right or wrong in his accusations, Mr. Trump has coined a new term here.

2. No, "fake news" is a term that can first be attributed to the Nazis of Germany. When Hitler first came to power it was with a promise to make Germany great again, and he endeavoured to keep that promise by fair means or foul, shaping the country into his kind of Germany. He did not like the criticism that often arose in the press. He called it "lugenpresse" meaning 'lying press,' and applied it to any media outlet that he deemed to be unsupportive of the Nazi party and its aims. The Nazi theory was that if you said something vehemently and often enough, even the non-gullible will eventually come to believe it.

3. This is actually a term of Canadian origin. Back in the mid 19th century each major political party had its own

newspaper or chain of newspapers. These papers were not at all backwards about supporting their own party and attributing all sorts of nasty things to political opponents. If a little bit of fabrication snuck into their reporting they didn't much care as long as it couldn't be proved and it wasn't so blatant that they might be sued for libel.

4. No, "fake news' has been around for centuries and the originator of fake news stories was very highly placed indeed. In the 13th century BC, Rameses the Great spread lies and propaganda portraying the Battle of Kadesh as a stunning victory for the Egyptians; he depicted, on the walls of nearly all his temples, scenes of himself smiting his foes during the battle. When the Hittites, against whom this battle was fought to more or less of a stalemate, disputed his claims of a "stunning victory" he accused them of lying, of, in effect, being purveyors of "false news" themselves. There was no press involved, of course, but he didn't care the source. Those who disputed his claims he made sure were labeled liars.

TWELVE

You've heard the phrase "to butter someone up." It means, of course, to flatter someone. But where did it originate and what's the connection?

1. It came from the colonial kitchen. Turkeys were traditionally coated with butter prior to roasting. It was thought to help render tough old birds more tender. Similarly, flattery was thought to help render "tough old birds", in the form of grumpy and cantankerous colonials, more tender.

2. Originally a French phrase, It relates to butter's ability to melt at relatively low temperatures, reminiscent of the way words and compliments flow so quickly and easily from the flatterer's mouth.

3. An ancient Indian custom involved throwing balls of clarified butter at statues of the gods to seek favour.

4. In ancient Rome, butter was a rather expensive but much sought after commodity. It was common practice to gain favours from corrupt officials by bribing them with small pots of good butter.

5. The phrase has actually not been around for an exceptionally long time. It is a Hollywood creation originating in an early Abbot and Costello movie. The scene involved the comedy duo being feted and treated royally by a tribe of South Sea Islanders. The two were tremendously pleased by the treatment until they were asked to strip

down so that they could have butter spread all over their bodies. It seems the islanders were a group of cannibals who wanted to "butter up" their guests prior to roasting them over an open fire.

THIRTEEN

You've heard the term "paint the town red"? It refers, of course, to a wild night out. And how did it originate?

1. It dates back to 1837, when an English Lord and his friends descended on a small English town to do some serious partying. The aristocrat, a known lush and mischief maker, went all out this evening. He and his friends ended the night with some serious acts of vandalism. Somehow they came across a supply of red paint, and began using it. They painted, gates, doors, and even a swan statue. They were drunk and acted accordingly.

2. It was April of 1896 and a by-election was being held in a small town riding, not far from Toronto. It had been a Conservative stronghold for over thirty years, and there was no reason to believe it would change that night. Unbelievably, it did. The Liberals unexpectedly won. Electoral maps would no longer paint the town a Tory blue. They would now show it as Grit red. Liberal supporters partied loud and long, and the next day newspapers across the country were carrying the story of how the Liberals had "painted the town red."

3. In 1924 a group of builders had won what they thought would be a lucrative contract for the construction of a "factory town" around a newly built automotive factory in rural Ohio. A small print clause in the contract, however, made them responsible for any unexpected costs for materials something that would normally be shared with

the industrialist. Well, there were some, and they were significant. They sued, but their legal challenge was thrown out of court, and the factory owner refused to help with anything. They were stuck. There was nothing in their contract, however, about the colour of paint that they were to use, so they chose a bright, garish, barn red, and painted every new building in town that very colour. They could no longer celebrate their lucrative contact, but they could at least celebrate getting at least some revenge on the greedy factory owner, and they did.

4. Back in 1921 movies were strictly silent and filmed in black and white. That year a western was being filmed and a set had to be built. Executives in the new film capital of Hollywood wanted to make a good movie, but they wanted to keep costs down too. One of the crews working on the set discovered that they could get a tremendous deal on paint, if they weren't too fussy about the kind of paint. The executives told them to go for it. The set was only going to be temporary, and with black and white filming, that meant colour was of little or no importance. To thank their alert crew, the execs arranged for a little partying with liberal amounts of liquor being supplied. The next day the workers "painted the town red." Newspaper carried the story, and that descriptive phrase was one that they used..

FOURTEEN

Here's a quickie for you. Might be an easy one too... or maybe not. "Prairie oyster"—a prairie delicacy. What is it?

1. A large, edible mushroom.

2. Regular oysters, shipped to the prairies, but served using a prairie recipe, based on the use of wild rice.

3. A large, freshwater clam found in some of the larger lakes of Canada's northern prairies, predominantly in the provinces of Manitoba and Saskatchewan.

4. Bull testicles cooked to perfection (assuming you can cook bull testicles to "perfection.")

FIFTEEN

You and two or three of your friends have planned a week in the outdoors. You'll be doing a little bit of boating, a little bit of hiking, a little bit of fishing, and lots of camping. One of your friends has brought a creel. What is a creel?

1. A wristband made up of paracord that can quickly be unraveled to provide one with an extremely sturdy, but lightweight cord that can be used in all sorts of emergency situations.

2. A wickerwork basket worn on the back or suspended from the shoulder, used especially by anglers for carrying fish.

3. A small, medication dispensing device in which needed medication can be placed in separate compartments that are reached through openings that can be accessed through a rotating cover that exposes those openings. Useful for keeping track of a number of pills that must be taken on a daily basis.

4. A portable water filter that uses osmosis to cleanse even some of the most polluted water sources in order to provide potable water.

5. Trick question! None of the answers are correct because, in reality, there is no such thing as a creel.

SIXTEEN

"Powwow". Today it is linked to aboriginal culture, and is associated with such things as dancing, singing, celebrating, gathering, eating, rodeos and the sharing of traditions. But was it always such? What is the origin of the term "powwow?"

1. The term "powwow" is actually a North Eastern Woodland word belonging to the Narragansett Language and the closest English translation is "meeting."

2. The term "powwow" is actually a Navajo word, and it referred more to a place than to an event. The closest English translation is "place of sacred ceremonies."

3. The term "powwow" originated with the Oglala Sioux of the Great Plains, who spoke a dialect of Dakota. The closest English translation is "treaty making."

4. The term "powwow" believe-it-or-not, is actually of non-aboriginal origins. It was born on the Canadian Prairies and was a term coined by the whisky traders from Fort Whoop-up, which was located in what is now central Alberta. They used it to describe the festivities they sponsored which included the shooting of a cannon, fireworks presentations, feasting and liberal use of cheaply made liquor—all in an effort to impress and encourage their indigenous guests to barter away the furs and pelts that they had gathered during the past year.

SEVENTEEN

There is only one country in the world without any mosquitoes, snakes, or other reptiles. That is...

1. New Zealand

2. Ireland

3. Iceland

4. Antarctica

5. Mongolia

6. Denmark

EIGHTEEN

The official London residence of the British royal family is Buckingham Palace. Why is it called `Buckingham 'Palace?

1. The answer is obvious. It was built for Britain's monarch in 1703 in Buckinghamshire, a small shire or province that has long since ceased to be, having been absorbed by the growing city of London.

2. Henry VIII confiscated the property upon which the palace currently sits from a Catholic nobleman who refused to recognize Henry as the spiritual head of England. At the time it was largely rural in nature. One of the few buildings that did exist was an Inn whose sign was that of a pig with rider, and known as the Bucking Ham. It was soon razed, but is remembered through the name that it left behind to be applied to the king's estate that was built in its stead. Beginning as a relatively smaller country residence, it was expanded greatly as the years passed.

3. Originally named Buckingham House, it was designed and built for the 1st Duke of Buckingham and Normandy. In 1761 the family sold it to King George III for £21,000. His wife, Queen Charlotte, had much admired the property.

4. King William II, of the House of Hanover, became the new monarch when the unpopular James II was deposed following England's "Glorious Revolution" of 1680. James had

a summer palace named Osborne House. King William, of course, became the new owner. He took up residence there and renamed it Buchenham Palace in honour of his birthplace in Holland. The name was later anglicized.

NINETEEN

English speaking peoples have a strange habit. They raise cows and pigs, but when they slaughter those animals and eat the meat, they do not eat cows and pigs. They eat beef and pork. Why is that?

1. Wrong! There is nothing strange about that. The same thing is done in almost all other languages. English speakers are not alone in the practice.

2. It dates all the way back to Celtic Briton. Druidic belief was such that when animals (and humans too for that matter) died they gave up their souls. Giving up their souls meant they became just a piece of meat. Thus, they were no longer cows and pigs, for they ceased to exist as such. Now they were known as "beef", "pork", and so-on.

3. Blame the Normans. When Wiilliam the Conqueror came to England, he did what he was known to do, and that was conquer. The Normans, in their role as an occupying people, changed a lot of things, including the language and the concept of dual names for the same creature.

4. The practice came into existence at the time of the great English drought of 1347 to 1349, which combined with the arrival of plague (the "Black Death" 1348 to 1350) led to famine in the land. Fields, if they were worked, provided only the scantiest of harvests. Herds and flocks were slaughtered wholesale in order to provide food and allow survival. When better times finally arrived, crops could be

regrown fairly quickly, but domesticated food animals had virtually disappeared from the land. There were some sheep for England which, at the time, depended heavily on the wool trade for revenue. As for other animals.... For many years meat for consumption had to be imported in the form of dried and salted meats. Foreign merchants, as might be expected, called their meats by the names they used back home—such as beef and pork. The practice was adopted by the English, and was continued even after English herds were eventually replenished.

TWENTY

"Out of the blue." That, of course, refers to something totally unexpected that has happened. And what were the origins of that particular expression?

1. An old, old term, perhaps dating back to Roman times, "out of the blue" references the weather. Occasionally a calm, pleasant summer day characterized by blue skies and few clouds, is suddenly transformed into a summer storm, with thunder and lightning unexpectedly appearing "out of the blue," and taking everyone by surprise.

2. It dates from the First World War, when, for probably the first time in history, battles were fought in the sky. German fighter pilots were probably the first to develop the tactic of attacking from above, flying high and diving down on unsuspecting allied pilots flying below them. German aviators liked to have the sun behind them to further disadvantage their enemy. British pilots described these attacks as something "out of the blue," referring, of course, to the skies above.

3. The phrase was first used during the "7 Years War", or as some have called it, the "French and Indian War." In the New World the British vastly outnumbered their French opponents, but the French tried to make up for that by traveling far and attacking unexpectedly. Settlers and military were generally surprised and usually dismayed when the bright blue uniforms of attacking French soldiers

suddenly came into view. Sudden danger arrived "out of the blue," as they described it.

4. Air mail proved to be a great benefit to a great many people. News from family and friends now arrived in just a few days (or in some cases, just a few hours) instead of a few weeks. Letters were usually written on special, light weight, blue paper, and enclosed in similar envelopes. The sudden and usually unexpected arrival of such welcome correspondence came to be described as news coming "out of the blue."

TWENTY-ONE

"To fly off the handle." That is said when someone loses control and can't contain his or her anger. The origins?

1. This dates back to pioneer times. Clearing of the land was done by axe and saw. Often axe handles were home made. If not made properly, or if not properly attached, the axe head might come flying off the handle when in use—a dangerous, inconvenient and maddening event.

2. This relates to the "horseless carriage." Vintage autos were once started by inserting and turning a handle into the crankshaft at the front of the car. Normally a fairly straight forward operation, one still had to be careful. Once the motor sprang to life the handle was supposed to disengage, but occasionally, especially when not held properly, the crank handle might instead fly out of the motorist's hand with such force that bones could be broken or other injuries result. "Flying off the handle," as might be expected, could produce both injury and anger.

3. "Handle" was the name given to a detachable platform that could be attached and removed from the side of a horse driven wagon. Old fashioned "snake oil salesmen" would stand upon this to demonstrate their wares to the assembled crowds. It was not unknown for hecklers to be a part of those crowds. If the heckler was persistent enough, and if the salesman's boiling point was low enough, the seller would sometimes "fly off the handle" and, in a fit of anger, go after the annoying heckler.

4. In "days of yore", fry pans were solid metal. They lacked insulated handles, meaning care had to be taken in using them. To remove them from the heat, a towel or some other sort of insulating material had to be used in order to safely grab that handle. Forgetting to do so would cause the cook's hand to immediately "fly off the handle" once it came into contact with the very hot metal. Burns might result, often accompanied by a string of profanities directed against the offending frying pan.

TWENTY-TWO

"An arm and a leg". Something that costs "an arm and a leg" is supposed to be quite expensive. And the origin of that phrase?

1. It first seemed to have been used during the Crimean War. Veterans of that war would often return home with limbs having been amputated—a very high price to pay for someone who was simply trying to serve his country.

2. It relates to 20th Century advertising. Store owners began adopting the practice of using "torso only" mannequins. Mannequins with arms and legs cost a lot more.

3. This phrase originated in the 18th Century and related to the painting of portraits. To keep costs down, those commissioning such artwork would request that no limbs be shown. Artists simply charged more if arms and legs were included in their artwork. That increased the complexity of the paintings being done.

4. This phrase originated in the late 19th Century and is a cousin to the phrase "a hollow leg", referencing someone who had the ability to consume a lot of alcohol. Big drinkers found the habit to be a costly one. Filling a hollow leg could be an expensive proposition, and it cost even more if there was more than one "hollow" limb that required filling.

TWENTY-THREE

"How did the word 'gossip' originate?"

1. It comes from the language of the Romani, the gypsies. "Gossip" literally translates as "story teller." The negative connotations related to the word probably stems from the fact that the gypsies, deservedly or undeservedly (no judgment is being made here) had a reputation as terrible liars and spreaders of falsehoods.

2. Thank Henry B. Gossup for bringing this word into being. A late 18th Century, unrepentant gambler, he particularly loved the horse races. He also had a little bit of the con man in him, and had a knack of having stories circulated about sick or injured animals, stories, usually false, that he used to increase the odds in his favour. Very successful at this at first, others in the "gaming industry" eventually caught on to his tactics, and warned others not to listen to "the gossup," whether it came directly from Henry or from others that he coerced or coaxed into spreading such rumours.

3. Politicians of old had to depend on feedback to find out what was important to people in their jurisdiction. They did this by sending their assistants out to the local taverns and pubs where most of the people hung out. They would sip some ale and listen to people's conversations, thus learning what was on people's minds and what their concerns were. They basically were told by their employers to "go sip some ale", thus the term "gossip" was coined.

4. This one goes way back. It is a direct descendant of the Old English word "godsibb" meaning sponsor or godparent. It was common practice for women to gather when births or baptisms were taking place, times when godparents were being selected, as these were ideal occasions for visiting and informal chitchat. Those engaged in such idle, familiar or trifling talk eventually came to be known as "gossips."

TWENTY-FOUR

Interested in some Canadian trivia? Here's a little trivia challenge with a Canadian slant to it. Which of the following was NOT invented either by a Canadian or in Canada?

1. The zipper

2. The pacemaker

3. The cordless phone

4. The tank (as a weapon of war)

5. Peanut butter

6. Basketball

7. The walkie-talkie

8. The garbage bag

TWENTY-FIVE

"Well, I'll be a monkey's uncle!" According to Wikipedia, this phrase "is used to express complete surprise, amazement or disbelief. It can also be used to acknowledge the impossibility of a situation, in the same way that 'pigs might fly' is used." And how did this term originate?

1. It dates back to Lord Byron, the much traveled English writer and aristocrat. After one of his lengthy sojourns abroad, he returned home to meet his sister's children for the first time. He was not impressed. He found them rude, rowdy and generally obnoxious, especially his oldest nephew. When a newspaper reporter asked him about this recent meeting with his family, he was quoted as saying that to his surprise, he had discovered that he was "a monkey's uncle."

2. Organ grinders are not as common as they once were. They were individuals who earned a living by their "musical presentations" that were accompanied by a trained monkey performing and collecting money from passersby. One of these organ grinders passed away and he bequeathed his organ and monkey to a cousin with whom he had long lost contact. It turned out this cousin was a very staid, very proper businessman. The newspapers had a field day describing how this pillar of society had suddenly become a "monkey's uncle." The phrase spread from there.

3. The phrase began as an insult. It was originally a sarcastic remark made by creationists who were adamant that the theory of evolution as advanced by men such as Charles Darwin was absolutely preposterous. The very thought that men descended from apes was considered blasphemous.

4. The phrase began as a compliment. Gibraltar, the British colony located at the southern tip of Spain allowed the monkeys native to the area, free run of the colony. If a troop of the animals were to take up temporary residence on your property, that was considered a very lucky event indeed. Such a fortunate individual could (as long as the simians remained there) call himself a monkeys' uncle. Good fortune, it was believed, would surely follow.

TWENTY-SIX

July 4th, Independence Day, is a huge holiday in the U.S. Likely, everyone knows why it is celebrated, but why is it celebrated on July 4th?

1. That is the day in 1776 when the Second Continental Congress voted to approve a resolution of independence declaring the United States independent from Great Britain's rule.

2. That is the day the Declaration of Independence was ratified and signed.

3. July 4th was the date in 1775 when Virginia became the first of the 13 Colonies to declare its independence from Great Britain. One by one the other colonies followed suit, maintaining July 4th as the anniversary date. July 4, 1776 was the first such National holiday.

4. The American forefathers were looking ahead. They wanted an official day of celebration in honour of the founding of their new country, and they wanted it in the summer when it would be most conducive to hold such a celebration. The first Sunday in July was chosen by the Second Continental Congress to be that date with Sunday, July 4, 1776 being the first such. Later it was decided to not worry about the day and to assign July 4th as the permanent date.

TWENTY-SEVEN

Let's look at the Model T Ford. It's famous. Probably everyone has heard of it. But why was it called the Model T?

1. In the early days of the auto industry, car models were not given fancy names. The original Model T was simply a Ford Touring Car. It was called the Model T in order to shorten the name, and it was done rather informally.

2. The public came to name the Model T. There was no contest, and there was no call to find a name for the vehicle. Someone had nicknamed it the "Tin LIzzie", and someone else described it as the Model T in recognition of that nickname. No one really knows who those some-ones were, but the name stuck. Both consumers and the company came to call it the Model T.

3. Henry Ford's youngest son was Thomas Ford. The elder Ford named his new automotive creation in honour of that son—hence, the Model T.

4. The Ford Motor Company made use of the alphabet to identify its car models. The first of those models was the Model A. The next was the Model B, and so on. By the time that they got to the Model T, it was replacing the Model S.

TWENTY-EIGHT

Did you use your cell phone today? Just about everyone has one. Why do you call it a cell phone?

1. It mimics the functioning of a living cell. It is free to move about. It is self-powered. It has a nucleus in the form of computer circuitry, and it can communicate with and work with other cells to form a more complex entity (a network).

2. The first "cell" phones were designed to provide wireless communication within American federal prisons. This gave prison guards much more mobility and a safer means of communication within the institution. It didn't take long to determine that they could be very useful in many other settings and they quickly moved beyond prison walls, although the original name was maintained.

3. The phones work in a "cellular network", which network is distributed over land areas called cells, so named because of the resemblance to the hexagonal shape of a honeycomb cell. The first "cell" phones were wired. Later models were wireless.

4. It is an abbreviation of the original concept name: Communication Equipment Lacking Linkage, meaning wireless operation.

TWENTY-NINE

We can fly on jumbo jets, eat jumbo shrimp, or, occasionally, dine on French Fries that are said to be in packages that are jumbo sized. It refers to the fact that something is much larger than normal. How did this word enter the English language?

1. It dates back to the Elizabethan era when the Spanish introduced a massive warship called the "jumbeau" which carried twice the armament of the English navy's largest war vessel.

2. "Jumbo" was actually the name of a very large and very famous elephant that American entrepreneur and showman, PT Barnum, purchased from the London Zoo in 1881.

3. "Jumbo" was indeed the name of a very large elephant, but not a real one. Jumbo was the name of Dumbo's father in the 1941 Walt Disney cartoon classic.

4. "Jumbo" was a pure fabrication. Heinrich Schroeder was a hot dog vendor who plied his trade on America's Atlantic City Boardwalk in the 1890s. He sold a massive hot dog that quickly became a customer favourite. He decided to call it the "Jumbo Dog." Why "jumbo"? He just thought this fabricated word sounded large and impressive.

THIRTY

P.T. Barnum was definitively the owner of a circus elephant named Jumbo, and it was a very famous elephant at that. But what was the beloved animal's ultimate fate?

1. Once it was time to retire Jumbo from his show business career, the elephant was resold to the London Zoo where he remained until his death in 1904, passing away from what they simply termed "old age."

2. Jumbo died in the 1892 Peoria, Illinois circus fire that killed the elephant and a great many other circus animals.

3. Jumbo died near St Thomas, Ontario in 1885 when a freight train collided with the massive animal, which died within minutes of the mishap.

4. Jumbo took ill and died during an 1890 sea voyage to France, where P.T. Barnum was planning to begin a European tour for his circus, with Jumbo slated to be the star attraction.

THIRTY-ONE

Some might say, "Chop chop", as in "You kids better hurry up, chop chop." If you said it, what did your mean and where on earth did that strange term originate?

1. It dates back to the building of Canada's transcontinental railway. American Cornelius Van Horne was appointed President of this, the Canadian Pacific Railway. He was not too demanding, but he was demanding. He expected his workers to work. The railway had hired a lot of Chinese labourers. That presented a language problem. To overcome it, Van Horne used a chopping gesture with his hands. That visual cue meant, "You better speed things up or you're fired." Supervisors and crew foremen followed his lead. Those Cantonese speaking workers might not have known much English, but they soon learned the meaning of "chop chop".

2. "Chop chop" is a phrase rooted in Cantonese, although the original term was "chok chok". It was a term used by Chinese workers in the South China Sea and was one which was adopted by English seamen. "Chop chop" literally means "hurry hurry" and was indicative of the need for something to be done now and without delay.

3. "Schnell schnell" is a German phrase. It was a term used by German sailors in the late 19th Century and was one which was adopted by English seamen. "Schnell schnell" literally means "fast fast" and was indicative of the need for something to be done now and without delay. When

the Great War broke out, it was deemed inappropriate to continue to use this German based phrase and it was ordered "chopped" from the vocabulary of English speaking sailors who substituted, appropriately enough, "Chop chop".

4. This dates from the early 1930s. In the depths of the depression the American Federal Government established work camps for the unemployed. Work was hard and salaries were meager, but meals were provided and it kept one from starving. These camps were generally established in national parks and other such areas where land needed to be cleared for the building of roads and other infrastructure. It became a practice, when daylight had arrived, breakfast was done and the time had arrived to get out and start removing trees to simply announce, "Chop chop." It was simple and effective and translated into "Grab your axes and hurry up to get to work!"

THIRTY-TWO

"Fuddle Duddle". That was a phrase uttered by an English speaking leader that was widely reported at the time, but hardly remembered now. Who said it and why?

1. Queen Victoria enjoyed her visits with Canada's first Prime Minister, Sir John A. Macdonald. She was less impressed with the dour Alexander Mackenzie, who replaced him. When asked about her conversation during the first and only time she visited with the new prime minister, she described it as all "fuddle duddle." It was a phrase that she admitted to manufacturing, but she thought it very descriptive or how "very boring" their conversation had been.

2. Teddy Roosevelt, as American President, was very supportive of the idea of National Parks. He found anti-environmentalists, who were more interested in exploiting than preserving to be beneath contempt. He described their arguments against the idea to be a bunch of "fuddle duddle", which, he explained, meant nice sounding platitudes, but ones with no real application to what was being discussed.

3. Winston Churchill was asked to comment on a rambling half hour speech made by the leader of the Labour Opposition who was arguing against one of Prime Minister Churchill's initiatives. He was quoted as saying his opponent's entire speech could be summed up in two words that he invented for the occasion, "fuddle duddle",

meaning nonsensical and consisting primarily of nothing more than hot air.

4. Canada's Prime Minister, Pierre Trudeau, was accused of having used some very unparliamentarily language (meaning unprintable) in speaking of an opposition member who he found to be very annoying. The Prime Minister addressed the accusation by stating that he may have moved his lips, but he actually said nothing. That didn't satisfy the press reporter who wanted to know what the PM was thinking when he moved his lips. Mr. Trudeau's exasperated reply: "Fuddle Duddle".

THIRTY-THREE

The next trivia challenge: "Loophole". A loophole, of course, is defined as a way of getting out of something or legitimately escaping what seems to be an insurmountable difficulty, especially finding some sort of a legal technicality that allows you to evade compliance. But why "loophole?"

1. The original loophole dates from in the middle ages. It was a small slit-like opening found in a castle wall. Here soldiers could fire their bows or musketeers shoot their muskets through these small openings in what seemed to be a seemingly impenetrable wall. They were not very large, but they were large enough for a child or small adult to squeeze through. Thus, a loophole is a small opening, or "out," that might be used if needed.

2. Originally written as "loupe hole," the name arose out the sometimes great difficulty in escaping contracted responsibilities. A loupe is a jeweler's magnifier, and it was said that it might take that careful an examination of small print in order to discern possible "outs" or "holes" whereby an escape from those contractual obligations was possible.

3. In the 17th and 18th centuries carefully groomed mazes were very popular additions to the grounds of estates owned by the well-to-do. To navigate the many avenues and loops to get from one side to the other could take some doing. Owners of these mazes would often arrange

to have carefully concealed "loop holes" constructed in order to facilitate early extrications if needed or wanted.

4. The original "loupe holes" were breaks in reefs that were too small for normal vessels to navigate. In South Seas regions local fishermen used small fishing boats called "loupes" that could get through these relatively small openings. Eventually the term loupe hole came to describe the sometimes hard to access and hard to find means of escaping difficult situations.

THIRTY-FOUR

Trifecta is now commonly known as a horse racing term for a bet in which the first, second, and third place finishers are chosen in the correct order. But why "trifecta"?

1. It was originally a medical term used to describe the three treatments used to treat the more serious cases of infection—purging (inducing vomiting), bleeding and the use of leeches. Practitioners had to admit that this was done only as a last resort, and was usually unsuccessful. The term was applied to racing since those betting on a trifecta were usually unsuccessful in their efforts.

2. This is a very easy one really. The "tri" in "trifecta", of course, means three, and the last part of the word comes from "perfecta" a word of American Spanish origin that refers to a horse-racing bet in which the first and second place finishers are chosen correctly.

3. Although a relatively recent addition to the English language, the concept has been around since the time of the Romans. The Romans, however, were betting on the chariot races, and in what is now known as a trifecta they would, indeed, try to predict first, second and third place finishers. A scholarly horse owner from Kentucky read of the practice, and thought that might work on the American racing scene. It did. "Trifectum" is what it was called in Latin. "Trifecta" is what they called it in English.

4. Originally a yachting term, a "trifecta" was simply an invitational race in which only three boats would compete. It had nothing at all to do with gambling. Horse racing enthusiasts, when they came up with the idea for the trifecta, must have had among them someone who had been familiar with the nautical term and liked the sound of it, for it was "borrowed" and used to name their new betting initiative.

THIRTY-FIVE

What is or was a vomitorium?

1. The vomitorium was a ward in a 19th Century hospital designated for the care of those suffering from (putting it as delicately as possible) stomach problems.

2. In late 19th Century and early 20th Century America, the vomitorium was that portion of a hospital set up for the treatment of human waste (of various sorts) prior to its actual disposal.

3. In Ancient Rome the vomitorium was a room adjacent to the dining area of Roman Villas. There banquet guests, who could not eat even a mouthful more, would retire to empty their stomach contents into awaiting earthenware jugs so that they could return to that dining area and continue with the banquet.

4. A vomitorium was a passageway in an ancient Roman amphitheater or theater that allowed patrons access to the rows of seats awaiting them. A series of such passageways were designed to rapidly fill and empty these places of entertainment.

THIRTY-SIX

Dandelion! It's a weed, but it can be a very pretty weed. Where did it get its name?

1. The beautiful, yellow flower of the dandelion reminded early settlers of a lion's mane. Apparently, it also reminded them of a "dandy". At the time of the naming a dandy was defined as someone who dressed with dignity but with a very great stress on appearance. Hence: dandy lion.

2. A 17th Century botanist named the flower after having carefully studied and classified it. He must have wanted his name to go down in history as he was very self-serving in the naming. The botanist in question was Daniel David Lyon (Dan D. Lyon).

3. The plant was named by the Beothuk people of Newfoundland. The Beothuks are long gone, and their language lost to the mists of history, but it is believed the meaning of the word was "flying flower."

4. Believe it or not, the dandelion is not native to North America. It is an invasive species, originating in Eurasia. The French called it "Lion's tooth" (dent de leon). English settlers maintained the name but anglicized it.

THIRTY-SEVEN

At one time if you wanted to take in a movie, you might say you were going to the flicks. Why "the flicks?"

1. Early cinema technology was not that good. It was not uncommon for a noticeable flickering to appear on the screen as the reels of film were pulled through the projector, hence the name.

2. This was in reference to the many serials and "shorts" that accompanied the main features. They tended to "flick" back and forth between these segments, hence the name.

3. This was in reference to the American agency authorizing the release and distribution of these movies. On the screen would appear the agency logo along with the wording, "Federally Licensed for Interstate Cinema."

4. A flick is defined as "a light sharp jerky stroke or movement." In the era of silent movies, pianists were hired to provide music to accompany the showing of these films. The need to suddenly change tempos and tunes was reminiscent of this flicking. movement. The term came to be applied to the movie itself, a term which persisted even after sound came into vogue.

THIRTY-EIGHT

If someone were to accuse you of being a spelunker, would they be praising you? Insulting you? What would they be accusing you of being?

1. A teller of tales, a bearer of false news.

2. Someone who illegally tries to manipulate elections.

3. A cave explorer.

4. A musician with an expertise in obsolete stringed instruments.

5. A newspaper proof reader whose specialty was to search out spelling errors.

6. An investment broker dealing primarily in mining stocks

THIRTY-NINE

If something is "cut and dried" (sometimes said "cut and dry") that means something is very clear, is set, or requires no discussion. What are the origins of this phrase?

1. It is a medical term. Basically, it is saying that a cut has been experienced, bleeding has occurred and a scab has formed. No further treatment is required.

2. This is a phrase which evolved in the 17th Century. It refers to the fact that a lawyer had drawn up a contract, the parties had signed it, and the ink upon it had dried. It was now over and done, or "cut and dried."

3. When dueling was legal, if someone felt slighted or insulted and a challenge was issued for a duel, time was allowed for apologies to be issued. If that time had passed and no apology was forthcoming, it was determined that the insult had been made (the "cut"), the time to apologize had lapsed (it had "dried") and there was now no going back.

4. This refers to the growing of herbs for sale. Once they have been cut and dried, that is it. No further growth is possible. The processing of this particular batch of herbs is done.

FORTY

Over the years a number of countries have ceased to exist as countries. Sometimes they go out of existence entirely. Sometimes they amalgamate with an existing nation. Sometimes they enjoyed a brief independence from another land but are later reabsorbed into it. Sometimes they are split asunder and form two or more new nations. Here is a flag of a once independent country. Of which was it or is it the flag?

1. The Falkland Islands

2. The Channel Islands

3. The Kingdom of Hawaii

4. The former colony of Newfoundland

FORTY-ONE

For centuries there was no Germany. There was, instead, a number of smaller kingdoms and states that were sometimes called "The Germanies". The most powerful of these, if you exclude Austria, which did not seem interested in German unification, was Prussia. In 1871 Prussia succeeded in creating one new nation out of many, and that became Germany. Wilhelm I of Prussia was crowned emperor. Austria, although also German speaking, remained a part of the Austro-Hungarian Empire, so was not a part of the Greater Germany that some envisioned. The trivia question: Where is Prussia located?

1. What a stupid question! Prussia, of course, is in Germany.

2. What Prussia? There is no Prussia.

3. Prussia is in Poland.

4. Prussia is in Russia.

5. Prussia is in Austria.

FORTY-TWO

These days we talk about laser guns, laser surgery, laser treatments, laser pointers and all sorts of other things laser. Where did the name laser originate?

1. It's actually an acronym. L.A.S.E.R. stands for Light Assisted Sinewave Emitting Radiation.

2. It's actually an acronym. L.A.S.E.R. stands for Light Amplification by Stimulated Emission of Radiation.

3. It's actually an acronym. L.A.S.E.R. stands for Low Amplitude Stimulation of Energized Radiants.

4. It's actually NOT an acronym. L.A.S.E.R. stands for absolutely nothing. The name was coined by a Sci-Fi fan scientist who named the discovery after a so-called energy weapon depicted in a Buck Rogers movie serial of the 1930s. The movie had called it a laser gun, a gun that shot laser rays instead of bullets.

FORTY-THREE

Golf. It's a very popular game, but what a weird name. From whence did it come?

1. Originally called "badger ball" from the similarity of its target holes to badger holes, it was imported into England from its home in Scotland. It immediately became a hit among the rich and privileged, but it was also found to be a producer of some very profane language by those playing. Such language was deemed inappropriate for the ears of the fairer sex, and women began to be excluded from badger ball courses. Course entrances began to have signs posted reading G.O.L.F.—Gentlemen Only, Ladies Forbidden. Badger Ball games soon became Golf games.

2. Golf was originally simply called "stick ball." King James II of Scotland was an avid player, but also a very bad one. He was also a very poor loser, and losing a match left him in a very foul mood. When feeling that way, it became very noticeable that he was much more likely to call for a flogging of common folk when meting out punishments. As a result his aristocratic fellow players began to call the game FLOG in honour of the inevitable results. In order not to further anger the king, however, in his hearing they would reverse the letters and call it GOLF. Its informal name eventually became its formal one.

3. Some ingenious Scotsman (It has not been possible to identify exactly who that was) attempted to describe

the exact sound made when the club hit the ball. To his ear it sounded like "GOLF" and he and others began to describe the act as "golfing the ball." Soon enough the game itself began being called a golf game.

4. The Scots may have perfected golf, but its origins predate Scotland. The name of the game is thought to come from colf or kolf, names for the clubs used in these early stick and ball games that were once played in Continental Europe.

FORTY-FOUR

Some more Sports Trivia. Tennis. You know of the sport. You know of the name. But where did that name originate?

1. It seems the game can be traced back to the monasteries of 11th or 12th Century northern France. There the monks developed a handball game called "jeu de paume" or "game of the hand." As time passed, rules evolved, and racquets came to be used instead of the hand, "jeu de paume" was replaced by the more modern name "tennis". Tennis seems to have come from the old French word "tenez" which could be translated as "take" or "receive" and is what one player would yell to his opponent as he served the ball.

2. Developed by the English sometime during the late 16th or early 17th centuries, the game's rules were somewhat complex and involved points, games, sets, matches and tournaments Racquets were used, and to differentiate the game from other racquet ball games, this one was called "Ten Set Racquetball", a name derived from some of those original rules. This was abbreviated as 10 S. As might be expected, rules, court sizes and so-on have changed considerably over time, but the name, in a sense, was maintained, although it came to be written as "tennis".

3. Tennis has North American origins. The basic game was played by the indigenous peoples in what eventually became the American state of Tennessee. English settlers came to play it as well, and British soldiers introduced

it to Britain when they returned home after service in the Colonies. They called it "tennis" in honour of its New World origins. Interestingly enough, the game basically disappeared from the USA shortly after the American Revolution. It had to be reintroduced from Europe.

4. Tennis has very ancient origins. It appears to have been developed by the Phoenician settlers of North Africa who founded Carthage, that great rival to Rome. When Carthage fell and was destroyed, the game remained. When the one-time Roman province of Tunisia fell to the invading Muslim armies, refugees fleeing to Europe took the game with them. It began to be called "tennis", a slight modification of the Tunisian capital's name of Tunis.

FORTY-FIVE

We sometimes accuse someone of "cutting corners," meaning he or she is saving on money by using cheap materials or skimping on proper attention to details, with the possibility of unsatisfactory end results. Where did the phrase "cut corners" originate?

1. It comes from the construction industry. Someone who "cut corners" was someone who eliminated rooms from a building under construction, leading to lower costs due to a decrease in the amount of material required, but considerably lowering the value of the finished product.

2. It was a driving term referencing the practice of not going all the way to a corner to make a turn, but instead heading off diagonally "cross country", saving on time but increasing the possibility of damage to your vehicle or accident with another.

3. It's a tailoring term, referencing using odds and ends of material (generally the "corners") stitched together instead of using a solid piece of fabric. This saves on money, but results in an inferior quality garment.

4. It's a printing term. "Corners" were the boxed ads that would appear in newspapers and magazines. Eliminating them lowered printing costs and increased speed of publication, but it also meant lost revenue, and revenues that were too low could lead to a possible closure, and a definite loss of profits.

FORTY-SIX

If something is said to cost a "pretty penny", it is meant that it is very expensive. But why "pretty penny"?

1. A penny was a common coin of low value, and not very attractive at that. A "pretty penny" came to refer not to pennies, but to the higher value silver coins. Thus, a claim that something was going to cost a "pretty penny" meant you weren't going to get it with mere copper pennies. Instead you would be resorting to the use of those higher value coins.

2. The term originated with numismatists or coin collectors. At first it only referenced one cent coins or pennies, but eventually it was used to describe any coin of noted rarity and uncirculated condition. Such coins, of course, could be quite expensive to purchase.

3. The term simply illustrates how the English language can change over time. One of the meanings of "pretty", a century or two ago, was "not a few" or "considerable." Thus, if you were going to say that something was going to cost a "pretty penny" you were actually saying that it would cost "a lot of pennies."

4. Contrary to what one might think, the phrase "a pretty Penny" originally did not refer to coins at all. It was, instead. A slang expression denoting a high priced prostitute, where a "penny" was a slang term for a prostitute. Consequently, if you were to suggest that something was

going to cost "a pretty Penny" you were really saying that it was likely to cost as much as you could expect to pay to obtain the services of one of these ladies of the night, and that, of course, could be quite a sum of money.

FORTY-SEVEN

Someone who is said to get "hot under the collar" or to be "hot under the collar" describes someone who is prone to fits of anger, an anger that this individual often has trouble controlling. What is the origin of this idiom?

1. Anger literally causes temperatures to rise. This results in faces and necks becoming red, sweaty and hot. Since collars cover the neck, collars too become hot and sweaty. Thus, the origin of the phrase.

2. The phrase originated in Puritan New England, and was a prediction as well as an observation. Those who could not control their tempers were likely to end up in the stocks. When the collar of the stocks was lowered onto their necks they could go nowhere and do nothing except feel the sun beating down upon them as they got "hot under the collar."

3. This was a 19th Century term coined to describe white collar workers who looked good, but whose business-like attire merely hid a quick to anger temperament. Employers, who preferred employees who were cool, calm and collected when dealing with the public, referenced this as being "hot under the collar," and often found this as grounds for dismissal.

4. It was originally a police term. When criminals were captured or "collared" by the police they tended to not be

happy about it. It was generally angry individuals who were thrown into jail. Anger results in rising temperatures so those who demonstrated that trait were described as "getting hot under the collar."

FORTY-EIGHT

Well, it is time to face the music, or at least it is time to analyze "it is time to face the music," for that is the idiom that is under consideration for this next trivia challenge. We know that it means accepting the truth and the consequences that go along with that acceptance, but what are this phrase's origins?

1. It dates back to the dance contests that were all the rage back in the 1930s. Contestants could remain boastful, hopeful and optimistic up until the music started. Then it was time to actually show their skills and prowess on the dance floor. Bragging would no longer be enough.

2. In America's Deep South of the Antebellum era, and even thereafter, cotillions were very important social events, especially for certain young men who wanted to impress certain young ladies. When the musicians began to play and it was time for the dancing to begin, it was also "time to face the music," as the saying went, and hope for the best.

3. The American Civil War was a bloody and tragic affair, as most wars are. This idiom arose during that conflict. Defenders knew that when the cannon barrage started and the enemy buglers began to sound, there was an attack commencing. It was then "time to face the music" where you would turn towards the direction from which the bugles had sounded and hope that your next few moments would not be your last.

4. The phrase dates from the mid 19th Century and comes from the British military. When someone was court-martialed and sentence was about to be imposed, there would be a military drum squad playing. Hence, "time to face the music," and find out what, if anything, the sentence was to be.

FORTY-NINE

"Ye Olde Tea Shoppe". We've probably all heard of or seen shops and stores who carry names reminiscent of the English of the Middle Ages — or at least reminiscent of the spelling used in Medieval England. What about the pronunciation? How should this phrase be pronounced?

1. The words should be sounded out exactly as written: Ye Oldie Tea Shoppie.

2. Actually, in those earlier years, there was really no such thing as standardized English. Consequently, you would properly pronounce this as "Ye Old Tea Shop". "Ye", of course, is now very much out-of-date, and is no longer a part of the English language, except, or course, in this attempt to hearken back to "Old English."

3. The letter "e" added onto old and shop really makes no difference, but whoever started this trend of using old-fashioned English (and it seems to have commenced in the 19th Century) obviously wasn't very familiar with old-fashioned English. "Ye" is the now obsolete plural form of "you", so the phrase properly spoken should be "You Old Tea Shop." That really doesn't make much sense, but blame the original user of this "Ye Olde" idea for that fact.

4. Modern English has dropped one letter from its alphabet. That is the letter "thorn" which was spoken with a "th" sound. In written form it very much resembled the letter "y" which is what might have confused the originator of what

some have called, "this cheesy form of advertising." As a result, the phrase should simply be spoken of as "the old tea shop." The extra "e's" were simply a spelling variant, and make no difference to the pronunciation.

FIFTY

Has anyone ever given you a "heads up?" That means, of course, that you were being given an advance warning, an admonition to be ready and wary. Where did the term "Heads up!" originate?

1. A carnival side show game developed during the 1920s and 1930s in which the heads of little creatures would pop up in a series of holes in front of a player. They would remain up only momentarily, and during that brief interval the player was to strike the creature with a wooden or rubber mallet. Enough correct strikes would win a kewpie doll, a small stuffed animal, or some other token prize. The game would begin when the barker would yell out a warning, "Heads up!"

2. It appears to have originally come into use in the early 19th Century. It was not a good idea for soldiers to nod off and start to doze while on duty. In fact, they weren't to even appear to be on the verge of doing so. "Heads up!" was the warning used to command them to remain alert and to remain looking alert.

3. Believe it or not, this was a hunting term. It came into vogue in the late 19th and early 20th centuries, a time when duck hunting developed as a very popular sport. It was common for hunters to go out in groups where they could do a little visiting and conversing while waiting for their prey to appear. When a flock was seen to fly over, someone would yell, "Heads up!" to advise everyone

to turn their gazes skyward, to grab their guns and to take aim.

4. The phrase appears to have first been regularly used by the Edison Studios, the motion picture company (1894-1918) founded by Thomas Edison. Department Heads would post updates relating to shooting schedules, staffing needs, and suchlike on a large company billboard. Staff were expected to pay regular attention to such notices which they began to call the "Heads' Update," or, abbreviated, as "Heads' up." The term soon spread to the general public.

FIFTY-ONE

The Alaska Highway links the current American state of Alaska to the Continental United States. It was a joint Canadian-American project that was rushed to completion during World War II. Why was it "rushed" to completion? What was the prime reason for doing so?

1. Started in 1938, it was felt that much time and money would have been wasted if work was stopped mid-stream, so it was decided to do all that was possible to hasten the finish so that valuable resources could be turned to the war effort.

2. Many thought that a Japanese invasion of the West Coast was inevitable, and the general consensus was that it would take place in the north. Having a highway system in place would facilitate the movement of troops and supplies to those areas most at danger, and, once the invasions had begun, to stem it as quickly as possible

3. Japanese submarines and surface ships were wreaking havoc with shipping in the North Pacific, and difficulties were being experienced supplying bases and garrisons in the Alaskan Territory, and conversely, getting mineral resources from Alaska to the south. Rushing to completion an inland road network would eliminate the threat from the Japanese Imperial Navy.

4. The Soviet Union in its life and death struggle with Nazi Germany was desperate for supplies and equipment. The

Atlantic sea route was fraught with dangers, as was the Pacific sea route. The relatively short distance between Alaska and Siberia made this an ideal way to get those needed supplies over to the USSR. Massive amounts were, in fact, needed. But how to get them there? A completed land route (the Alaska Highway) would solve that problem. Thus the haste.

FIFTY-TWO

Have you ever owned a "briefcase?" Many people have. What, however, is the origin of "briefcase?"

1. This one goes way back, all the way back to Roman Britain, in fact, The Britons used an etched leather bag for the carrying of valuables. The Romans were impressed with it, and began copying the design and using it themselves. "Brefa" was the Celtic word for leather. Hence the origin of the "brief" case.

2. In the late 18th Century tourism began to grow in popularity, at least among the well-to-do. Leather workers began to cater to this market by designing bags and other carriers for the travellers' clothing. This is where suitcases came to be. Smaller bags were developed to handle smaller items such as toiletries and a quick change of clothing. Since underwear was often a part of that change of clothing, these came to be called "briefcases."

3. In the late 19th Century traveling salesmen took to the railroads to sell their wares across the country. Accompanying them were their sample cases. Larger cases would usually contain a number of samples to show their customers. Smaller cases were usually limited to a few small samples or none at all. Instead they would rely on pamphlets or small catalogues to show their customers. These catalogues contained brief descriptions of the items available for purchase. The salesmen called these cases their "brief cases".

4. We have the legal profession to thank for the term brief cases. Originally called brief bags, lawyers would use them to carry legal briefs. These briefs were summaries of the facts of a case, with reference to the points of law supposedly applicable to them. They were commonly brought to court by the attorney.

5. We have the military to thank for the term brief cases. Originally called briefing cases, senior officers would use these to transport confidential documents to meetings with junior officers and other staff. Kept locked and with a guard normally present, the maps and other sensitive materials contained within would be used, in confidence, to brief those present on anticipated actions, planned objectives, campaigns and maneuvers.

FIFTY-THREE

If someone were to say they "fell off the wagon." We would understand them to be saying, "I've started drinking again." Well, what is this "wagon" to which they were referring?

1. The saying started off as "I'm on the wagon." Before that it was. "I'm on the water wagon." Water wagons were wagons that carried water to dampen roads and keep the dust down. Thus, "I'm on the wagon" could be translated as, "It is strictly water for me now." Consequently, to be off the wagon meant the decision for "strictly water" was gone by the wayside.

2. The phrase can be linked to the Temperance Leagues that fought so strenuously to end the use of alcoholic beverages. The leagues held many a parade with the "newly converted" being given the privilege of taking a seat in a horse drawn wagon bedecked with signs advertising the fact that they had taken "the pledge." Not all of the "newly converted" stayed converted, however, and when they rejoined their friends in the beer hall it was often with the announcement that they had "fallen off the wagon."

3. The police tried to keep the highly inebriated off the streets. To aid their efforts they would load these drunks into a police paddy wagon to be taken to the police station drunk tanks, where they would remain until sober. Naturally, when they were in the wagon, they were forced to refrain from drinking. Once they were "off the wagons" and back in the street that restriction would rapidly disappear.

4. Breweries employed beer wagons to deliver their production to their customers. Brewery owners, however, did not want any sampling going on while their "liquid refreshment" was being delivered. Consequently, a strict no drinking policy was put in place and rigidly enforced. Drivers, other employees, and the occasional passenger knew that these had to be "dry runs." Of course, once they had got down from the wagon and were on their own time, these restrictions disappeared. As they drank they referred to themselves as having "fallen off the wagon."

FIFTY-FOUR

If someone were to ask you, "Is this on the level?" they would be asking you if something was true, if it was accurate, or if you were lying to them. What is the origin of this phrase?

1. At one time, to be on the level also meant to be sober, to be clear-headed. Thus, asking if something is on the level was akin to asking if this was the result of fabrication, of muddled thinking, or of a somewhat tenuous grasp of reality.

2. The phrase refers to an old-fashioned jeweler's or goldsmith's scale. To gain an accurate assessment of a quantity of gold or some other precious commodity, both arms of the scale must be properly weighted and level with one another.

3. This relates to road construction. Roads need to be free of obstacles. To build them often requires the removal of trees and rocks. Some grading will probably be required. In other words the terrain needs to be leveled, and work can only begin when assurances can be made that everything "is on the level."

4. The phrase can be dated all the way back to the 14th Century. Stonemasons used squares and levels to make sure their work was properly done, with lines straight and surfaces true. Their use of "on the level" eventually spread to the general population.

FIFTY-FIVE

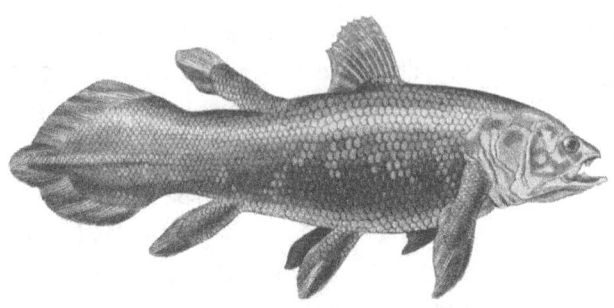

Drawing from: http://www.tomlytle.com/

Pictured here is a coelacanth, a primitive fish that thrived some 400 million years ago, but which scientists determined to have been extinct for at least 65 million years. Recent discoveries, however, have revealed something truly unique about this fish. What was this discovery?

1. It is believed to have been warm-blooded.

2. It appears to have been a transitional species, one that could live for short periods on land as well as in the water.

3. In tracing the origins of the science, it was found that its fossilized remains were among the first such to be discovered and studied, leading directly to the science of paleontology.

4. The "extinct" was discovered not to be extinct. It still exists in today's oceans.

FIFTY-SIX

"Hands up!" Many a Hollywood movie has depicted that command being used when someone was being stopped and being arrested, or stopped and being robbed. During the days of the English Highwayman, however, there was a different phrase commonly used. What were the well-known words that English travelers dreaded hearing?

1. "Sing for the King!"

2. "Reach for the Skies!"

3. "Prepare to be boarded!"

4. "Halt and extend!"

5. "Stand and Deliver!"

6. "Move and you Die!"

FIFTY-SEVEN

If we were to say that something was "over the top" we would be saying that this "something" was excessive, overdone, or simply too much. What are the origins of this idiom?

1. It comes from the docks. If a vessel was overfilled, it sat too low in the water and in even a mildly turbulent sea there was a significant danger of water coming "over the top" and having it flounder.

2. It comes from the saloon or the pub. Bartenders, at their peril, had to learn to not be too generous with their customers. If mugs and glasses were continually filled to overflowing, owners would declare the work of their bartending employees to be unacceptable or "over the top" and they would soon find themselves out on the street looking for other work.

3. It comes from the battlefields of the First World War. When it came time to attack, soldiers would have to leave the relative safety of their trenches and go "over the top", as they called it, to cross no-man's land and launch themselves towards the enemy positions on the other side. Losses were generally horrendous, and some thought "excessive."

4. It comes from the early days of television. Network censors were given lists from which they had to work. At the bottom of the list were depicted those situations, routines, and so on that were deemed suitable for showing during

daylight hours when little children might be watching. The middle of the list did the same for the early evening hours, when older children might be up, but little children were probably abed. The top of the list again did the same, but allowed a little more leeway since this was for the late evening hours where it was expected the audience would almost exclusively be adult. There were, of course, those situations, etc. that the censors would deem unsuitable for showing to anyone at any time. Television producers who attempted to exceed those bounds were accused of having gone "over the top," and were refused permission to broadcast.

FIFTY-EIGHT

There is a short poem: "Good night. Sleep tight. Don't let the bedbugs bite." Let's forget the bedbugs portion. What does it mean to "sleep tight?"

1. This phrase dates back to the days when mattresses lacked box springs. Instead, they were supported by ropes or straps; sleeping tight meant sleeping with those ropes pulled tight, which would provide a well-sprung bed, and a comfortable, sag-free sleep.

2. There was a time when saying someone was "tight" was synonymous with saying they were drunk. To wish that a person would sleep tight, was not to suggest they go to sleep inebriated. It was to wish them the sleep **OF** the drunk—sleeping soundly, sleeping deeply, and sleeping without any thought to worldly cares.

3. Though now considered to be generally obsolete, there is or was an adverb, *tightly,* meaning 'soundly, properly, well, effectively.' The phrase, then, should read, "Good night. Sleep tightly. Don't let the bed bugs bite." Of course, the rhyming would be spoiled by that, so 'tightly' had to become 'tight.'

4. To be transported safely, shipboard cargo had to be carefully stored and tied down. Things had to be "tight." It is this use of the word that pertains to the "sleep tight" idiom. The sleeper is being urged to sleep securely in a safe bed, knowing that all is well about them.

FIFTY-NINE

A former Canadian Prime Minister was also able to list "Nobel Prize Winner" amongst his list of accomplishments. Who might that have been?

1. Lester B. Pearson

2. Brian Mulroney

3. Louis St. Laurent

4. George-Etienne Cartier

5. Sir Robert Borden

6. Uh, oh, another trick question. None of Canada's prime ministers has ever won a Nobel Prize.

SIXTY

A "wild goose chase" is generally agreed to mean a hopeless quest, a "chase" that cannot be brought to a successful conclusion. Why that name?

1. A "Wild goose chase" was actually the name given a not so terribly nice practical joke. A group of friends would invite the victim to go hunting with them, promising that they were going to try and bag some flightless geese. The unsuspecting hunter would literally be given a large bag and told to lie in wait while his buddies went to chase a flock his way. Then he was to throws his bag over one of the geese that would come waddling by, and capture it live. There was, of course, no flightless geese and no chasing being done. The hapless victim would wait, and wait, and wait some more until he finally realized that this was nothing but a big joke, and he would have to wend his way home alone and in the dark.

2. This was a term used by British fox hunters. It referenced a fox hunt that had gone awry. No fox had been brought to ground, and no fox had been shot. They called it a "wild goose chase" because no matter how many hunters there were, no matter how many horses they rode, and no matter how many dogs they had to assist, no geese could be hunted in this fashion. They could not be "brought to ground". They would simply take flight and disappear. Consequently, it seemed a good name for and an apt comparison to an unsuccessful fox hunt.

3. To duck and geese hunters, "a wild goose chase" was something too ridiculous to even consider. If the geese either flew over without being shot or could not be lured down with decoys, they simply escaped the hunters' guns and were gone for good. There was no point in chasing after them in order to try again, for geese cannot be hunted in that fashion.

4. A "wild goose chase" actually had nothing to do with hunting. It was a horse racing term. At one time there was a type of horse race where the horses involved would follow behind a lead horse. The riders in the race traced the route being taken by the lead rider through an unpredictable course. Onlookers were reminded of flying geese in formation following (or chasing) a leader, thus the name. Of course, the object was not to catch the lead horse. It was always to follow the route being established.

SIXTY-ONE

If you were tired and felt you couldn't stay awake any longer, you might announce, "I am going to hit the hay," meaning you were going to go to bed. What does "hitting the hay" have to do with going to bed?

1. The phrase originated with American GIs fighting in Italy during World War II. If, at the end of the day, they were lucky enough to be able to attempt a peaceful sleep, the most likely place to achieve that was in some farmer's hay filled barn. The exhausted soldier would literally throw himself down into the hay in the hopes of getting some of that much needed shut-eye.

2. In the late 19th and early 20th centuries, people used to sleep on mattresses that were little more than cloth bags stuffed with hay or straw. Before they went to bed, they usually found it necessary to "hit the hay" in order to render the mattress at least somewhat more comfortable and perhaps to make sure there were no bugs inside.

3. This referred to the end of day practice once common on most farms where farm workers would climb up into the lofts of their barns where hay for their horses was stored. They would then hit, knock or throw down enough bales so that the hay could be used to provide fresh hay for their work animals when they were brought in from the fields at night.

4. "Hit the hay" began as a sports term. It was a time when professional football teams were beginning to come into being in the U.S. At training camps it became common practice to end the day with tackling practice. Straw or hay filled bags were used for this purpose. For the players in training to "hit the hay," as they called it, signified the end of training for that day.

SIXTY-TWO

If the observation is made that someone is still "wet behind the ears," we mean to say that person is inexperienced, immature or very naïve. But why "wet behind the ears?"

1. A comparison is being made to the inexperience of a baby, so recently born as to still be wet.

2. New soldiers entering battle for the first time tend to do so while sweating profusely in what is called a "nervous sweat". There is often enough perspiration to leave them "wet behind the ears," a sure indication of their inexperience.

3. Years back, bath night was a time when family members shared bath water. Mom and Dad would bathe first, followed by the children, beginning with the oldest and ending with the youngest. Thus the oldest family members got to enjoy the cleanest, warmest water, and would be the first to get dried off. At the end of the evening those whose hair remained damp and who were still "wet behind the ears" would obviously be the more junior members of the family.

4. This references a young man so young and inexperienced that he has just begun to shave. Like any other daily process there is a bit of a learning curve involved. Perhaps because, at first, one might not towel off properly, these young men were often said to be "a little wet behind the ears," alluding to missed bits of shaving soap.

SIXTY-THREE

It is still a tradition for some, that when a couple is newly married, the groom is to carry the bride over the "threshold" the first time they enter their new home. That raises the question, "What is a threshold and how did it get its name?"

1. The original meaning of "thresh" was "to tread" or "to trample". Consequently, the threshold, which is a wood or stone sill located at the base of doorways, got its name from the fact that those entering a home would tread upon, trample upon, or step upon it as they came into the dwelling.

2. Medieval homes often had a threshing room located at the front of the house where grain could be threshed during inclement weather. The activity gave its name to the doorway sill.

3. Medieval homes were frequently a part of a farmyard. Being so close to the straw and other debris that would litter the ground in a typical farmyard, a gust of wind could easily bring it through open doorways and into a home. A wooden plank placed across the doorway (literally a "threshold") would help to prevent this.

4. Medieval homes featured dirt floors. Homeowners or tenants would often cover these floors with whatever suitable materials they could find — straw reeds, rushes, or whatever. Frequently chosen were 'threshings,' the straw left after grain was threshed. The objective, of course,

was to keep this inside and not allow it to drift outside. A wooden plank placed across the doorway (literally a "threshold") would help to prevent this.

SIXTY-FOUR

To be "saved by the bell" is to be given a last minute reprieve. Why the term "saved by the bell?"

1. This idiom dates back to the late 18th and early 19th centuries. Exhumation of some graves provided evidence that there had been some people who had been buried alive—probably due to the misdiagnosing of coma as death. This discovery resulted in the development of safety coffins, coffins in which the occupant, should he or she awake after burial, could cause to have rung a small bell above ground that would indicate that the corpse was not really a corpse — thus, "saved by the bell."

2. In the early 20th century buildings began to be built that incorporated fire alarm systems in the design. It proved to have been a brilliant idea. It didn't take long at all to prove that the ringing of fire alarms saved both lives and property — thus "saved by the bell".

3. Boxing developed into a tremendously popular sport. Bells were used to signal the end of rounds. On more than one occasion fighters, who seemed on the verge of losing, were given at least a brief reprieve by the round coming to an end — thus "saved by the bell."

4. This one dates all the way back to the time of Viking raids on the coast of England. Coastal villages found it wise to appoint watchmen to watch for the arrival of Nordic invaders. Should they discover a raid was taking place

they would have the local church bell ring out a warning, allowing the village inhabitants to either fight or flee, as seemed appropriate —thus, "saved by the bell."

SIXTY-FIVE

Some people work what is called the "graveyard shift," which is an early morning / late night work shift. Ever wonder how it got that name?

1. Back in the middle of the 19th Century rumours began to spread about some people mistakenly being buried alive. Certain coffin makers, in order to cash in on these worries, came up with cleverly designed "safety coffins" in which occupants, should they come to consciousness after being buried, could cause a bell to ring or a little flag to wave above ground. Of course, in order for this to be effective, someone needed to be around to hear the bell or see the flag moving. That wasn't such a problem during daylight hours, but it was during evening hours. Consequently, special watchers were hired to be on hand "just in case." This came to be known as the graveyard shift.

2. The term originated with the San Francisco Police Force in the late 1890s. It was observed that the murder rate seemed to be at its worst during the hours after midnight and before sunrise. Officers working those hours came to call it the "graveyard shift," The papers soon picked up on it, and from them it spread to a usage by the general public.

3. In the latter half of the 19th Century a general belief arose that a work shift commencing after midnight was not good for you. It was felt that those working such hours

became more prone to sicknesses or even premature death. Consequently, such shifts came to be called "graveyard shifts."

4. It seems the "graveyard shift" was born out of "graveyard watch." The first usage of that term began appearing in the late 1890s. Sailors began referring to the 12:00 am to 4:00 am watch as the graveyard watch because their ships were usually "deathly quiet" during those hours and those were the hours in which disaster was most likely to strike, When the term began being used on land, "watches" were switched to "shifts."

SIXTY-SIX

Over the course of the centuries many new breeds of dogs have been developed, but many others have gone extinct as well. Pictured above is one of those extinct breeds, the Salish Dog. Native to Canada's British Columbia and Washington State in the United States, these dogs disappeared in the 19th Century. They had primarily been prized for one unique reason.

1. They were fed a special diet of fresh and cooked salmon which was thought to render their flesh most tasty. They were considered a true delicacy among the Indigenous people who raised them.

2. They were fed a special diet of cooked and fresh fish, which was thought to be very good for their coats. Like sheep, they were sheared once a year with the resultant wool being used in the manufacture of ceremonial blankets.

3. They seldom barked, but when they did it was with a uniquely high pitched yelp that was considered to be extremely effective in driving off evil spirits.

4. The aboriginal peoples who raised them thought they made wonderful pets. Cute and cuddly, they were extremely loyal to their owners.

SIXTY-SEVEN

Pewter is an alloy consisting mostly of tin which has been mixed with small amounts of other metals such as copper to harden it and make it more durable. It is an attractive metal, inexpensive enough to make it an economical choice for use in the production of all sorts of household and other goods. Artisans of the Roman Empire excelled in its use. A wide assortment of vases, kettles, tableware and cooking pots were in wide use, especially during the latter stages of the Empire, and in all but the humblest of homes meals would be eaten off pewter plates, using pewter cutlery with the food having been cooked in pewter pots. Current thinking of many experts has it that pewter had a significant role to play in...

1. ...the enriching of Rome through its trade in pewter with Persia and other kingdoms and empires to the east.

2. ...the development of metallurgical industries within the Empire.

3. ...Julius Caesar's decision to begin the conquest of Celtic Britain as he sought control of the island's great tin deposits.

4. ...the fall of Rome due to a fault in Roman kitchenware that made it far inferior to that of other nations.

SIXTY-EIGHT

A "peeping tom" is a person with voyeuristic tendencies, someone who spies on other folk through keyholes, windows, the slats in a fence and so on. The "peeping" part is obvious, but why "Tom?"

1. This relates back to the time of Lady Godiva's famous ride. Legend has it (and it probably is only legend) that all the townsfolk respectfully averted their eyes when the great lady rode by, that is all but Tom the Tailor who couldn't resist a quick peek or two when she rode past him.

2. This references the Apostle Thomas who wouldn't believe that Jesus was resurrected until he actually saw for himself.

3. The term "peeping tom" came into existence in honour of Sir Thomas Boynton (Lord Salisbury), the great Elizabethan spy, who visited the Spanish Court and reported back to his Queen on many of the hitherto secret plotting of the Spanish monarch and his advisors.

4. We can thank Mother Goose for this one with Tom, the Piper's Son, being the inspiration. At one time verses included descriptions of him spying on naked ladies and their lovers. Those verses disappeared in the 19th Century when the poems were cleaned up to make sure they were suitable for family reading. However, the term "Peeping Tom" persisted.

SIXTY-NINE

"To Steal (One's) Thunder" has been defined as "To steal one's idea, plan or intellectual property and use it for profit or some benefit." (Farlex Dictionary of Idioms. © 2015 Farlex, Inc.) How did this come to be called "stealing one's thunder?"

1. John Dennis was a 19th Century horse breeder. He had a magnificent steed named Thunder. However, in 1848, the horse was stolen from his Kentucky stables. The authorities were not able to apprehend anyone. The next year he was visiting relatives in New York, and they attended the races being held at the local race track. He was dismayed to find his animal, now racing under the name of Lightning, not only running in but winning one of the races. He brought charges and a sensational trial followed.

2. John Dennis was a playwright who, in 1933, was contacted by a Hollywood studio to be the screenwriter for a new movie about to go into production. After it was finished he returned to his home in the east. It wasn't long after its release that it became apparent that the movie was proving to be a huge box office success. John immediately made plans to return to the west where, he told his friends and family, he expected to be welcomed with "thunderous applause". Instead he learned that one of the producers had taken credit for the writing of the script, and he hadn't been given even the minutest bit of acknowledgement. After sharing his story with the newspapers, he filed suit.

3. John Dennis was an 18th Century actor-manager-playwright, and in 1709 he wrote a play in which the sounds of thunder were needed. No device existed to make such noise, so he invented one. Unfortunately for him, the play flopped. His company moved on and another one took over the theatre for their production. It happened to be 'Macbeth'. John attended the play and was aghast to find that, without permission and without acknowledgement, they were using his thunder device. He was very public in denouncing them.

4. John Dennis was an automotive engineer who did a great deal of freelance work. In 1958 he approached Ford executives with a number of ideas that would help to super power their popular Ford Thunderbird. The end result was a redesigned body and the new 430 CID V8 motor. At least that is what he said he did. The ideas worked, but Ford claimed the design and engineering ideas did NOT come from Mr. Dennis. He sued, but lost. He sued again and lost. It total he brought Ford to court three times, and lost each time. However, he went to his death bed still claiming that they had stolen his "Thunder," his pet name for the vehicle.

SEVENTY

Francis (Frank) Jeffrey Dickens (1844-1886) was the fifth child and third son of the famous author, Charles Dickens, and Catherine Hogarth. In 1874 he came to Canada. Why?

1. He came to court, propose to, and then marry Heloise Langevin, a daughter of Hector-Louis Langevin, one of the Fathers of Confederation. He had met her during a visit the family had made to London, England. After their marriage, he returned with her to Great Britain.

2. He came to join the newly organized NWMP (Northwest Mounted Police).

3. He came to take over as editor of the *Kingston Expositor*, a newspaper founded by family friend, Henry Blackwood.

4. He had been appointed Lieutenant Governor of the recently organized Province of Ontario and came to take up his duties.

SEVENTY-ONE

Woodrow Wilson, President of the United States of America, was president during the First World War. When the war ended he envisioned a world where the tragedy of such major conflicts would never be repeated. America, then, led the way in advocating the establishment of an International organization that would provide a forum for peacefully resolving international disputes. Thanks, in large part, to the power and prestige of the president, and his unrelenting efforts to get other nations to share his vision, that organization was formed and it was named "The League of Nations" (precursor to the "United Nations"). Even though its membership grew over the years, it ultimately failed. There were many reasons for its failure, but one of the prime ones was that one very important country could not be persuaded to join. That nation was...

1. China

2. Great Britain

3. Italy

4. France

5. Germany

6. Japan

7. The USSR (Union of Soviet Socialist Republics)

8. The United States of America

SEVENTY-TWO

"Don't look a gift horse in the mouth." That is the saying, and most people seem to be aware of its meaning. You should not insult the gift giver by trying to assess the value of the gift that you have received, whether it be that of a horse or something else; rather you should be thankful for the thoughtfulness shown in the giving. When it comes to horses, however, why would you want to look in its mouth anyway?

1. It is not so much the looking as it is the attempt to look. A well trained horse will allow its owner to look in its mouth. A poorly trained horse will resist.

2. You look in a horse's mouth not so much to see what is there as to smell what is there. Certain diseases give a horse's breath a distinct odour. If those odours are present, that is a good indication that the animal is ill.

3. A look in a horse's mouth can reveal signs of abuse. The one doing the examining would be attempting to see what kind of a bit has been used, and whether or not the horse has been injured as a result of that use.

4. You look in a horse's mouth in an attempt to determine its age. A trained observer can be fairly accurate in assessing the age of a horse by looking at its teeth.

SEVENTY-THREE

If someone was to say, "You let the cat out of the bag." he or she would be accusing you of revealing a secret. What, however, does letting a cat out of a bag have to do with disclosing a secret?

1. In the days before wire pet carriers were available to carry small animals, ordinary burlap bags were used. Thus, breeders and sellers of puppies and kittens would place the dog or cat in a bag for purchasers to take home. Unscrupulous sellers would sometimes secretly substitute mongrels or common alley cats for more expensive breeds, something the buyer might not discover until getting home and "letting the cat out of the bag."

2. In medieval markets it was common practice to sell "alive and kicking" livestock. Piglets, for example, were often sold in this manner. Tied in bags for farmers to take back home, shady dealers would sometimes substitute cats for pigs, a con that was discovered only when the farmer got home and opened the bag.

3. Gossips were often accused of being catty, of sharing confidences with which they had supposedly been entrusted. The best way of avoiding this was to avoid the sharing of such information with such people. Failure to take this preventative action would allow those gossips to reveal that which should have been hidden. In other words, you would have given them access to this

tantalizing bit of news, which, consequently, untied the gossip's tongue—"let the cat out of the bag."

4. Traveling side shows once had a simple game designed primarily for children. Various objects, and occasionally even live animals, were placed in a box or bag, hints were given, and the children asked to guess what was inside. Those guessing correctly would get some sort of a small prize. The guessing ended, of course, when the hidden contents were revealed, an action that came to be known as "letting the cat out of the bag."

SEVENTY-FOUR

"To turn a blind eye" to something is to knowingly ignore situations or facts or to show an inability or unwillingness to recognize reality. The origin of this idiom…?

1. It was popularized by a story relating to Britain's Lord Nelson. The British were engaged in a sea battle with a joint Danish/Norwegian fleet. The wary British admiral signaled Nelson to break off his attack. This was done by the use of signal flags. When informed of this, Nelson, who felt certain that victory was at hand, said he must see this for himself. Blind in one eye, he held the telescope that was handed to him up to his glass eye, said that he couldn't see any such signal, continued with the attack, and was victorious.

2. John Manwelling, a sports reporter for the *Pittsburgh Tribune* was, of course, an ardent fan of the Pirates baseball team. On May 23, 1923 he reported on a Pittsburgh loss that he didn't think should have been a loss. He was extremely critical of the officiating, conjecturing that the home plate umpire must have had one glass eye for he could see every mistake that the Pirates made, while "turning a blind eye" to calls that should have gone against their opponents.

3. The phrase had a German origin, dating back to the waning days of World War II. Hitler had begun issuing orders for military units that had long since been obliterated. No one dared contradict him so no one corrected

his now fanciful directions for impossible military maneuverings. After one such meeting Generalfeldmarschall Kesselring wryly reported to one of his aides that the fuhrer was obviously having some problems with his eyesight as he was "turning a blind eye" towards a reading of the military maps at his disposal.

4. Winston Churchill told the "turning a blind eye" story of a nameless heiress and the nameless, but financially challenged, aristocrat who married her. The gentleman had earlier confided to the future British Prime Minister that he considered her a "hideous hag." Churchill one day asked him if he would continue to describe her as such. The man replied, "Oh, no. I solved that problem long ago. Now, when I am in her presence I merely remove my glasses."

SEVENTY-FIVE

Hermann Goering; a Nazi military leader, Commander of the Luftwaffe (German Air Force), President of the Reichstag, Prime Minister of Prussia and Hitler's designated successor; had a younger brother, Albert. Albert was much less well known than his infamous sibling, but he was not inactive during the Second World War. What did he do?

1. He was one of the scientists involved with the Nazis' rocket program. He was still working feverishly to bring the V3 to readiness when Peenemunde (their research facility on the Baltic Sea island of Usedom) was destroyed by the Allied forces. He was later brought to the USA along with a number of other German scientists who helped found NASA, the American Space Program.

2. He generally worked in the background. Besides serving as a liaison officer, he was a speechwriter for his brother, for Rudolf Hess, and for other famous Nazi leaders. He was also thought to be one of the architects of Hitler's "Final Solution."

3. He proved to be a propaganda genius, serving under Joseph Goebbels until the end of the war. It was he who was largely responsible for orchestrating the Nazis' highly successful "Lügenpresse" or "Lying Press" campaign that served to undermine legitimate news reporting and mute criticisms of the Party.

4. He was a successful businessman who risked life and limb to save as many Jews and political dissidents as he could. When Austria became a part of the "Greater Germany" he even managed to have Archduke Josef Ferdinand of Austria, a Habsburg prince, freed from the Dachau Concentration Camp.

SEVENTY-SIX

To "click" with someone has been defined as meaning, "to sense an immediate connection, to hit it off at once, or to be quick in establishing a rapport with an individual." But what is generally agreed to be the reason behind the use of the word "click?"

1. It goes back to the days of analog tuning on a radio dial. The best reception is only established when you "click" on the right frequency.

2. "Click" started as a societal thing. You were most comfortable with people in the same "clique." Thus, "to click" or "to clique" with someone simply meant that someone was in the same circle of friends, with similar likes, dislikes and interests.

3. "Click" can be referenced to the opening of a lock. If you were to insert a key, turn that key, and hear a "click" it means it was the right key and you have established a perfect fit.

4. This is a relatively recent term originating in the computer age. Computer programs can be wonderful things, but to "click" with them, you must "click" on them, using your mouse.

ANSWERS

One — 2
Two — 1
Three — 4
Four — 1

Trivia on the Trivia: The Canadian successes were truly astounding. During those 100 days they actually saw one quarter of all Germany's land armies trying, unsuccessfully, to stem their advances. It should be noted, of course, that by this time morale was becoming a serious problem for the Germans, and they were finding it increasingly difficult to replenish losses of men and equipment, but that was still quite an accomplishment for a small country. Some say Canada's victories contributed significantly to a shortening of the war, with Allied leaders previously hoping that a successful conclusion to the hostilities could be achieved in 1919. Instead the official end to the war came on November 11, 1918. Sadly, the casualty lists were very high for Canada during these "one hundred" days, though, in the long run, their successes may have saved many more lives than were lost.

Five — 1
Six — 3
Seven — 2
Eight — 1

Trivia on the Trivia: In the Middle Ages, cats were commonly thought of as sinister beasts with basically the same powers as witches and warlocks, obviously in cahoots with Satan. A cat's bite was thought to be poisonous, as was its flesh, and if you breathed its breath, you'd be infected with consumption (also known as tuberculosis). They could also make your beer go sour if they felt like it. As such, when bubonic plague swept the European continent in the 14th century, killing up to 60% of the population in some regions, it was naturally assumed that the Devil was responsible, and his handiwork was attributed directly to his feline minions. Tremendous numbers of cats—especially black ones—were destroyed during this wave of the plague, and sometimes their owners along with them. (To be fair, snakes were also blamed and destroyed as well.) This was ill-advised, of course, because the real distributor of the plague was the Oriental flea, which lives on rats, and with dramatically fewer cats (and snakes) to keep their numbers in check, the rat population in Europe soared … as did deaths by the plague.

Nine — 4
Ten — 2
Eleven — 4

Trivia on the Trivia. Regarding question eleven, you might argue the correctness of that response by saying the term "fake news" hasn't been around for that long. Nevertheless, all of the stories told here are basically true, which means the term itself may be new but the concept has been around since ancient times.

Twelve — 3
Thirteen — 1
Fourteen — 4
Fifteen — 2
Sixteen — 1

Trivia on the Trivia: Although answer 4 was not the correct answer, the Fort Whoop-Up mentioned did exist. Its presence contributed to the formation of the North West Mounted Police (eventually renamed the Royal Canadian Mounted Police). Fort Whoop-Up was a destination on their march west in 1874. The American traders who manned the fort were operating illegally and little could be done to stop them since the Canadian Government lacked a functional police force in the area. Once the NWMP were on the scene, the sale of illegal, high-priced whisky largely ceased, and the complaints of Aboriginal leaders such as those of the Peigan Chief, Three Bulls, were addressed.

And from **Karen Shirley:** I promised I would provide an Indigenous people's perspective on the word "pow wow", so here is one. The origin of the word "pow wow" is so ancient that no-one can accurately identify its true origin. However, a couple of different North American Indigenous languages have words that sound similar: the Narragansett word (powwaw); the Massachusett word (pauwau). Both of these are Algonquin languages. From a non-Indigenous perspective, a Pow Wow is simply a multi-day, multi-generational, multi-cultural Indigenous gathering full of drumming, dancing, singing, socializing, food, and fun. From the Indigenous perspective, a Pow Wow is all of the above AND EVEN MORE ... it has strong sacred, spiritual aspects and strict protocols that must be met and followed. Before the Pow Wow begins, there will be pipe ceremonies and the grounds will be blessed to become hallowed ground. The sacred fire is lit in the centre of the "floor". It burns for the entire time the Pow Wow runs. When the drums arrive at the Pow Wow, the first place they must go is to the sacred fire with their drums. They bless the drum, warm it up, and say a prayer. The sound of the drums is the heartbeat of our ancestors and some say also the heartbeat of the earth. The sound of the drums will draw you in. Dancers arriving will also often first go to the fire and offer tobacco, in gratitude and to acknowledge their ancestors. After the Grand Entry and the head dancers are introduced (one of whom must be on the floor at all times and watch that all protocols are followed), the Traditional dancers come onto the floor. The rather plain regalia (very bland, often made of doeskin or other hides with light bead-work or other decoration) that they wear symbolizes their humility, the kind of humility that it takes to walk traditionally. Traditional dancers must become very spiritual once they start traditional dancing. They lead the first dance of the Pow Wow because they bring, invite, or welcome the spirits of the ancestors. They learn, know and bring the stories of the ancestors. Other dances, like the Jingle dancers, Grass Dancers, and Shawl dancers, have other spiritual meanings. The songs the drummers sing have sacred meaning. The Pow Wow is for prayer, sharing, respect, kindness, and open-mindedness. No anger, unkindness or other evil-doing is allowed to mar the hallowed nature of the Pow Wow. There are times when you don't take photographs or video during a Pow Wow. If the Master of Ceremonies (someone with a very full knowledge of the Pow Wow protocols and Orders of events and who is also usually the Announcer) asks the people to stand in honour of some individual or a group of people, photos or videos are not allowed. Should an eagle feather drop accidentally from one of the dancer's regalia, that is a big deal, and a special ceremony must be performed. An eagle's feathers are given to a dancer in honor, and the feathers are worn with dignity and pride. They are treated with great respect. When an eagle feather is dropped during a dance, a special ceremony is performed to pick it up again, and the owner is very careful to never drop it again. The eagle is a sacred bird because it flies so high, to the heavens and to the Creator. The people look to the eagle as the symbol of their prayers being carried to the realm of the Creator. The drumming, the singing, and the dancing are all forms of prayer to the Creator because you are doing it in a good way.

The Naragansett claim they have been holding Pow Wows consecutively each year for the last 343 years of their history.

Seventeen — 3

Trivia on the Trivia: Perhaps Antarctica as well, but Antarctica is NOT a country.

Eighteen — 3

Trivia on the Trivia: A little bit of an explanation may be in order, for the Normans did not intentionally cause this to happen. It was more a happening by happenstance. Normandy was French speaking, so William the Conqueror, as might be expected, spoke French, as did his fellow countrymen.. All of a sudden the majority of the English aristocracy were French speaking since the Normans were now "in" and the Saxons were now "out". When meals were served, they, of course, used the French terms. They didn't eat pigs. They ate "porc". (known to us now as "pork") They didn't eat cattle, they ate "boeuf" (beef). From time to time, they dined on sheep ("mouton"), which over the years became anglicized as "mutton". Somewhat similar tales could be told about veal and deer meat (venison). The common folk seldom saw such expensive cuts of meat appear on their tables. They did have access to some meats, primarily chicken and fish, which is probably why poulet (French for "Chicken") and "poisson" (fish) did not come to be used when referring to cooked meats from these species. As for pork and so on, even after French faded from the scene as the mother tongue of the English aristocracy and everyone began to consume these other meats, the English continued to eat pork instead of "cooked pig."

Nineteen — 3
Twenty — 1
Twenty-one — 1
Twenty-two — None of the above.

Trivia on the Trivia: In researching this phrase, most sources say the origins are "uncertain." One did say the painting of limbs aspect was the true origin. Another said that is pure fantasy. Yet another dated it from the American Civil War. Someone else said that wording, in a slightly modified form, has been around since at least the 1600s. And, another rumour has it that Henry Ford was the originator of the phrase. (I couldn't find that citation myself, but I have no doubts but that someone somewhere was adamant that this was the case.) Sadly, we may have to leave this one as "we just don't know".

Twenty-three — 4
Twenty-four — 4

Trivia on the Trivia: To many, the answer here seems obvious. Yet, it is not. "Although popular culture would have some believe otherwise, peanut butter wasn't invented by American botanist George Washington Carver, who was a huge promoter of the peanut as a soil enriching crop for the American South. To bolster demand he also diligently researched commercial possibilities. He ultimately developed 300 derivative products from peanuts—among them milk, flour, ink, dyes, plastics, wood stains, soap, linoleum, medicinal oils, and cosmetics. Peanut butter, however, was not amongst them. Rather, it was created in 1884 by Canadian pharmacist Marcellus Gilmore Edson, who likened the consistency of his product to that of butter, lard or ointment." He developed it as a health food. "Peanut butter," it was pointed out, "was invented to provide a nutritious food for people who couldn't chew solid food." The tank, the correct answer to this trivial challenge, was actually the invention of an Australian.

Twenty-five — 3
Twenty-six — 1
Twenty-seven — 4
Twenty-eight — 3

Twenty-nine — 2
Thirty — 3
Thirty-one — 2
Thirty-two — 4
Thirty-three — 1
Thirty-four — 2
Thirty-five — 4

Trivia on the Trivia: The *vomitorium* question may be a bit of a tricky one for some since there has been an "urban myth" circulating that there really was a room set aside in Roman households for diners to go and vomit. In reality: Not so. As for the correct answer, one source elaborates: "The vomitoria of the Colosseum in Rome were so well designed that it's said the immense venue, which seated at least 50,000, could fill in 15 minutes. (There were 80 entrances at ground level, 76 for ordinary spectators and 4 for the imperial family.) The vomitoria deposited mobs of people into their seats and afterward disgorged them with equal abruptness into the streets — whence, presumably, the name."
(www.straightdope.com)

Thirty-six — 4
Thirty-seven — 1
Thirty-eight — 3

Trivia on the Trivia: One source goes a little bit further and, in one of their definitions, claims, "If you ask people who actually go caving, spelunking is the derogatory term for stupid or unprepared cave trips. Origin: 'spelunk' is the sound a clumsy caver makes when he slips and falls in a cave and lands in water." (https://www.urbandictionary.com) Amusing, but probably not true, since "spelunk" is an obsolete term for a cave or grotto.

Thirty-nine — 4
Forty — 3

Trivia on the Trivia: Hawaii, once known as the Sandwich Islands, having been named such after the archipelago's discovery by Britain's Captain James Cook, was, at the time of discovery, ruled over by a number of competing kingdoms. It was in 1795 that King Kamehameha I, through a combination of warfare and diplomacy, succeeded in uniting the islands of Hawaii, Oahu, Molokai, and Lanai into a single government. By 1810 all of the islands had joined the Kingdom of Hawaii. At the behest of American business interests, in 1898, and to the chagrin of many native islanders, the United States annexed Hawaii. It became the 50th state of the Union in 1950. To this date a small, but vocal, sovereignty movement continues to advocate that the annexation be undone.

Forty-one — In a sense, all answers are correct except no. 5.

Trivia on the Trivia: To elaborate — "In 1945, after defeat in World War II, Germany came under the control of the victorious allies—the United Kingdom, the United States, the Soviet Union, and France. Northern East Prussia was annexed by the Soviet Union; the rest of the *Land* east of the-Neisse Line transferred to Poland; and the remainder was divided between the Soviet, British, and French zones of occupation. One of the few acts of the Council was the formal abolition of Prussia on February 25, 1947." (*https://www.britannica.com/place/Prussia*)

Forty-two — 2
Forty-three — 4
Forty-four — 1
Forty-five — 2
Forty-six — 3
Forty-seven — 1
Forty-eight — 4

Trivia on the Trivia: To be honest, not everyone agrees that this is the origin of the idiom, though most experts do. Coincidentally, the term "drummed out of the military" is also said to have come from this practice.

Forty-nine — 4
Fifty — 2
Fifty-one — 2
Fifty-two — 3
Fifty-three — 1
Fifty-four — 4
Fifty-five — 4

Trivia on the Trivia: This fish truly was thought to have been extinct. Quite dissimilar to modern fishes, it was in 1938 that a specimen was found in a fisherman's net drawn up by a trawler that had been fishing off the coast of South Africa. Since then Coelacanths have also been discovered off the Indonesian coast. If not extinct they are at least rare. Current species are inhabitants of the deep sea, and may be found at depths of some 2300 feet. They can grow large—a little better than 6 feet long and weighing almost 200 pounds. It is also said they taste horrible.

Fifty-six — 5
Fifty-seven — 3
Fifty-eight — 3

Trivia on the Trivia: There has been a common misconception that this idiom does, indeed, date from the era of "rope beds." It does not. Such beds did exist, but the "sleep tight" saying came into being well after their era of popularity had come and gone. Besides, as one online commentator attested, "'sleep tight' has nothing to do with rope beds. I live in an area with multiple historic buildings and the tour guides always come up with that line. When my kids were little, I bought a rope bed and used a feather mattress (we live in a historic house ourselves) and slept on it a number of times. Trust me, a tight rope bed is like sleeping on a knife bed. Give those ropes some slack! Hammocks aren't stretched out between 2 trees. They hang loosely between trees. Tight ropes on a bed are bad, very, very bad." (juliebird11 quoted in *http://www.word-detective.com/2008/08/sleep-tight/*)

Fifty-nine — 1

Trivia on the Trivia: Lester B. Pearson (1897-1972) was Canadian Prime Minister from 1963 to 1968. From *Nobelprize.org:* "In 1956, Great Britain, France and Israel launched an attack on Egypt aimed at removing President Nasser. The United States had not been informed, and the Soviet Union threatened to use atomic weapons against the assailants. The "Suez Crisis" found its solution when the Canadian Secretary of State for External Affairs, Lester Pearson, who had served as President of the United Nations General Assembly in 1952, won support for sending a United Nations Emergency Force to the region to separate the warring parties. This gained him the Peace Prize for 1957."

By the way, for anyone who picked Cartier, that was an okay guess if you are American. You probably don't know a lot of Canadian history. If you were Canadian, however, you should have known better. George Etienne Cartier was a prominent politician, but he was never a Canadian Prime Minister.

Sixty — 4. (The race was popular in Elizabethan England.)
Sixty-One — 2
Sixty-Two — 1
Sixty-Three — 1

Trivia on the Trivia: To be fair, it should be pointed out that there is not universal consensus that this answer to the question is correct, although most sources would agree. There is, however, almost universal agreement that there is some inaccurate information floating about. Several sources cited one specific article, "Life in the 1500s", that provided a definition of "threshold" very close to what was given here as answer number 4. According to Snopes: "In a nutshell, this article about "Life in the 1500s" is nothing more than an extended joke, someone's idea of an amusing leg-pull which began its Internet life in April 1999. All of the historical and linguistic facts it purports to offer are simply made up and contrary to documented facts:" Sadly, such articles give no indication that they have little or no basis in fact.

Sixty-Four — 3

Trivia on the Trivia: Pertaining to this question, it should be noted that there really were safety coffins, some of them rather elaborately designed, but the term "saved by the bell" did not originate with them.

Sixty-Five — 4
Sixty-Six — 2
Sixty-Seven — 4

Trivia on the Trivia: Roman pewter was alloyed with a number of other metals, but lead was a particular favourite, sometimes with the percentages reaching as high as 30 to 50%. High acid foods would leach out this lead, and, of course, lead which was leached out would be consumed with the meal. The Romans, it should be stated, were known to be high users of lead in all sorts of situations. Lead pipes were used to bring water into Roman baths and homes. Pewter and lead were used to flavour wine. Lead was found in make-up. There was even an artificial sweetener that gained its effectiveness through the use of lead. The rich and the powerful were the biggest users of the metal, and the use of the metal itself was increasing over time, meaning the rich and the powerful were consequently more and more likely than the general public to suffer from lead poisoning, and all of its deleterious side effects. For the well-being of the Empire, that was a bad thing. Lead poisoning can lead to organ failure and numerous other problems. As one online article based on research by the BBC (British Broadcasting Corporation) points out, "Considering that lead poisoning can cause miscarriage, reduced sperm count, (an) increase of violence, poor physical condition or even mental disorders, the situation wasn't appropriate for a conquering nation." (*https://historykey.com/lead-poisoning-ancient-rome/*)

Naturally, all of this gave an advantage to any of the enemies of Rome who, unlike the Romans, chose not to gradually poison themselves. Although in Rome some among their number were actually concerned about the overuse of lead in their society, the Romans, as a whole; since they lacked modern, scientific knowledge of lead and its tendency to slowly wreak havoc with one's health; were not too concerned about what the naysayers had to say.

To be fair, not all experts agree with this assessment, so anyone who failed to answer "4" to this question might have some justification in turning it down as a response. It is, however, an interesting theory is it not? And it does seem to be supported by a growing number of studies. Certainly, it may not have been the direct cause of Rome's fall, but many have now come to the opinion that it seems to have been a contributing factor.

As a final note: Roman conquerors did make use of British tin, but that was not likely the reason for Caesar's initial invasion. He seemed anxious to prevent a regrouping and counterattack by the recently-conquered Gauls who had escaped the victorious Roman armies by fleeing north to join their Celtic cousins, the Britons.

Sixty-Eight — 1
Sixty-Nine — 3
Seventy — 2

Trivia on the Trivia: Dickens did not make the grade as a police officer. Political influence got him into the Force as a sub-inspector, and he was later made an Inspector, positions which it seems were hardly merited. According to the *Dictionary of Canadian Biography* (Volume XI (1881-1890)). "Dickens was assigned to D division, then stationed at the temporary headquarters of the NWMP at Dufferin, Man. For the next six years he moved with the headquarters from Dufferin to Swan River Barracks (Livingstone, Sask.) and Fort Macleod (Alta), and finally to Fort Walsh (Sask.). To be kept under the eye of the commissioner this long could mean either that an officer was marked for promotion or that he was considered a bad risk for an independent command. Dickens' fitness reports leave no doubt that those in charge were reluctant to trust him. superiors consistently rated him as lazy, alcoholic, and unfit to be an officer in the NWMP."

He died 11 June 1886, having never married.

Seventy-One — 8
Seventy-Two — 4
Seventy-Three — 2
Seventy-Four — 1
Seventy-Five — 4

Trivia on the Trivia: The Goering brothers were quite a contrast, with Hermann being a true anti-Semitic, and Albert having no love for the Nazis, at one time describing the man that his brother idolized as "that bastard Hitler." Nevertheless, they were brothers and both considered familial ties important.

William Hastings Burke, Albert's biographer, described the situation:

"Albert regularly went to his brother's Berlin office to curry favour on behalf of a Jewish friend or political prisoner, manipulating Hermann's ego and playing on his sense of familial duty. In this sense, Hermann was a safety net for Albert. As Albert became ever more audacious in his subversiveness, a mountain of Gestapo reports piled up against him. Four arrest warrants were issued in his name during the war and yet he was never convicted. Big brother always came to his aid, however politically damaging it might have been.

"In 1944, a death warrant hung over Albert, demanding his execution on sight. He was on the run, hiding in Prague. Hermann dropped everything to save him. 'My brother told me then that it was the last time that he could help me, that his position [had] also been shaken, and that he had to ask Himmler personally to smooth over the entire matter,' Albert testified in Nuremberg." (extracted from: *Thirty Four,* Burke's book about Albert Göring)

Seventy-Six — 3

www.ingramcontent.com/pod-product-compliance
Lightning Source LLC
LaVergne TN
LVHW011840060526
838200LV00054B/4111